MW01253304

Veronica Trunzo continues to teach and write, and currently resides in Santiago, Chile. She was born and raised in Ottawa, Canada, and graduated with a degree in Art History and Literature from the University of Toronto. She is currently working on her second novel, *Pavla's Doll*.

Dedicated to Děde. Your adventurous spirit was with me throughout these adventures.

Veronica Trunzo

LIKE A LOTUS

Remember that life is an adventure!
Let me know where this book ends
up in the world ♡

— Veronica Trunzo

@ Author — Veronica Trunzo

@ trunzo_vtravel

AUSTIN MACAULEY PUBLISHERS™

LONDON • CAMBRIDGE • NEW YORK • SHARJAH

Copyright © Veronica Trunzo (2021)

All rights reserved. No part of this publication may be reproduced, distributed, or transmitted in any form or by any means, including photocopying, recording, or other electronic or mechanical methods, without the prior written permission of the publisher, except in the case of brief quotations embodied in critical reviews and certain other noncommercial uses permitted by copyright law. For permission requests, write to the publisher.

Any person who commits any unauthorized act in relation to this publication may be liable to criminal prosecution and civil claims for damages.

The story, experiences, and words are the author's alone.

Ordering Information
Quantity sales: Special discounts are available on quantity purchases by corporations, associations, and others. For details, contact the publisher at the address below.

Publisher's Cataloging-in-Publication data
Trunzo, Veronica
Like a Lotus

ISBN 9781947353329 (Paperback)
ISBN 9781643783888 (Hardback)
ISBN 9781641828925 (ePub e-book)

Library of Congress Control Number: 2021909703

www.austinmacauley.com/us

First Published (2021)
Austin Macauley Publishers LLC
40 Wall Street, 33rd Floor, Suite 3302
New York, NY 10005
USA

mail-usa@austinmacauley.com
+1 (646) 5125767

There are so many people, I need to thank for helping me bring this book to life. First of all, thank you, Austin Macauley Publishers, for believing in this story and making this dream of mine come true.

I would never be where I am today if it wasn't for my incredible family. Thank you, Dad, for always sticking by me and supporting all my dreams. Joey, you are the easiest person in the world to talk to and I hope you know I always have your back, like you've had mine. My amazing, Mom, thank you for the late-night phone calls, messages, and staying up listening to me read these chapters to you over and over again; you helped make this book happen. Babi, thank you for being the biggest fan of my writing.

There are so many people I have met along the way; I don't even know where to start and I don't think I can even mention everyone. To my girls in Cambodia; Kate and Sophia, and the ones I unfortunately failed to mention in the book: Donna, Lauren, Sarah, Laura, Jessica, Mimi, Sam, Rebecca, Evelien…and the many more I am missing, thank you for being my family abroad. I will hold the memories we share in my heart forever. You were part of the best times of my life.

My China family; Katie, Sam, Carmen, Francesca, and Molly. We made each other's days better. And thank you, Shawn, for being the best boss ever; I still miss our talks!

Of course, my best friends in the world: Mitch and Claire.

Mitch, my journey began with you. We have been on more adventures than I can even count. Thank you for all the moments I will forever cherish. I cannot wait to see what we do next!

Claire, this book would never have happened without you. I hope you know how amazing, inspiring, and supportive you are, and I will always be there to try to pay you back for everything you have done for me.

And thank you to everyone who took time to read my story; I hope it gave you inspiration to choose your own destiny.

"Travel changes you. As you move through this life and this world, you change things slightly, you leave marks behind, however small. And in return, life and travel leaves a mark on you."

– Anthony Bourdain

Prologue

My lungs are on fire.
They can barely fill up with oxygen.
My head feels like it's going to explode.
I don't think I can keep going.
But God is it ever beautiful up here.

I stood there looking over a valley full of grazing yaks, surrounded by giant snow-covered mountain peaks. My legs were shaking. My lungs were struggling for breath. My toes were throbbing. My eyes were full of wonder and amazement.

Occasionally, I had to just stop what I was doing, take a moment to absorb in the scenery around me, and wonder to myself: *How did I ever get here?*

Over the past ten years, I've lived in three different countries and traveled through more than I can count. Though, the most exciting part of it is: I did it on my own.

Home has become wherever I feel safe enough to sit back with my journals and spill my heart and soul out onto the paper.

I've been in awe, in shock, totally amazed, terrified, lost, in love, and completely full of wonder. I've been nostalgic yet determined to keep going. I've been exhausted and excited and everywhere in between. I've been doing it alone, and what's most frightening about that is, I don't think I could have it any other way again.

How did I ever get here?

Sometimes you just have to go back to the beginning to answer that question.

I've taken my heart-and-soul-spilled-out journals, my only constant companions on my journey, and mashed them together into this book. My only hope is that my story will fill your eyes with wonder, and your heart with curiosity, and in this harsh world, I hope you know; there is nothing you can't do.

Chapter 1

Canada

I'm going to start off my story in a typical, corny, overdone way; a girl's first heartbreak…I know, I'm sorry. But doesn't every adventure begin this way? Being forcefully thrown into the world alone, afraid, and with no other choice but to find strength in oneself?

I met Ray when I was eighteen years old, young, kind of shy, and inexperienced, and ready to fall head over heels in love; which is exactly what happened. No love is ever quite like your first one, is it? Your naivety and innocence open you up to love without any limits or boundaries and puts your heart out there like a blind man running through a minefield.

I was a university student with a head full of dreams, and Ray was a novice cop with a head full of ambition. He was handsome, kind, romantic, and strong; and damn, did I fall hard. I was studying art history at the University of Toronto, you know, one of those majors you take when you have no idea what you want to do with your life. But like most new high school graduates, I thought I would take on the world.

I met him at a college bar, one of those dark places where the floor is sticky, and the band is too loud.

He dazzled me right away.

"Can I buy you a drink?"

"Well, I already have one actually."

"Okay, how about a drink next weekend then?"

He smiled at me with those sparkling blue eyes, and I felt butterflies in my stomach.

"I think we can make that work."

And that was that.

Ray was always supportive of my University years, and in 2011, when I finally graduated, I left Toronto and moved out west to start our lives together.

That's when things got tough.

Ray had an amazing career, he was so full of drive and ambition, and from the beginning his job became his world. I don't blame him at all, to this day I am proud of his success, but I was stuck in our suburban home trying to figure out what the hell I was going to do with my life. I felt so young and so full of life. So many amazing opportunities ahead of me that felt just out of reach. I had the American dream at my feet; a beautiful home, a loving boyfriend turned fiancé later, a secure office job, money in the bank, and a cute dog with a white spot on her back. Wasn't that the full package?

For over a year I did everything right; I cooked healthy dinners every night, I walked our dog after work, I joined yoga classes and book clubs, tried to befriend other cops' wives, and I even volunteered at the hospital one summer. But God, was I unhappy. And the worst part was I had no idea why! Isn't this what we fantasized about as kids? Isn't this what we grow up for? I was so blessed, so fortunate, but God was I unhappy. I think what scared me the most was that my life seemed forever planned. I knew where I'd be five years down the road; ten years down the road.

To me, life was starting to feel pointless.

I approached Ray one morning before work.

"We haven't been anywhere in a few months; why don't we plan a vacation soon? Remember how we always talked about Mexico?"

Ray looked up at me from his uniform he was meticulously ironing.

"Babe, we just came back from that wedding in Banff a couple weeks ago. I thought you had a good time."

"Yeah but, I've got some money saved. We could afford a little hotel on the beach for a week. I still have some annual leave from work."

Ray walked up to me carrying his uniform, kissed me on the forehead, and proceeded to the closet to hang it up.

"Maybe we should save that for our wedding we haven't started planning yet."

I was left standing in the middle of our bedroom, feeling disappointed, guilty, and even up to this day, the most confused I had ever been.

***

The next few months are a blur. I spent all my days working at an office job I hated, and all my nights waiting for Ray to come home from either work, or from the bar with his coworkers. My days became a distortional haze of working, groceries, cleaning the house, walking the dog, and drinking wine in front of the TV.

Repetition. Day after day.

I had a hard time making friends, and all I wanted was to spend more time with my fiancé. He was all I had, and my desperation just pushed him further away.

He took on more shifts. He worked as much overtime as he could. He grew closer to the men and women whom he spent all his days with, and further away from the lost, lonely fiancé waiting for him at home. I began to resent his happiness. He had such a purpose. He had a wonderful reason to wake up every morning. He had goals and ambitions. He had a place in the world.

I, however, was lost, and alone.

He in turn, began to resent my unsupportive attitude. He didn't know how to make me happy anymore and didn't know where I fit into his life.

I became emotional, negative, and always on edge, and Ray, justifiably, became distant and closed off.

"Where have you been for the past two days, Ray? You're always working overtime or you're with your buddies, and I'm always left alone here!"

It was a cold, early November morning. I had been trying to sleep but was up all night waiting for Ray to come home. Like a broken record at that point.

"I was with Ben."

"Where? Why?"

"I needed space," he solemnly answered and turned around to leave.

"Come back here! Why are you always gone? You're never home!"

"Veronica, leave me alone. Go back to bed."

"Ray! Tell me right now, what the hell is going on?!"

He spun around to face me.

"I'm not happy! I'm not happy because you're not happy and I can't make you happy! I think I need a break."

He then walked downstairs, left out the front door, and I was left sitting in bed listening to the crunch of his car wheels drive down the snowy road.

And that was that.

The next thing I remember was sitting in the airport, waiting for my flight to Ottawa, with my engagement ring still on my finger. I was in such shock I couldn't even cry. It was my fault, I caused both of our broken hearts, but I still felt complete doubt. For over four years he was all I knew. He was my comfort, my stability, and my home. I was lost, and alone. My selfish desire for seeking what I was missing ruined that relationship.

I landed in Ottawa late one sunny morning, and as soon as I saw my dad waiting for me in arrivals, I finally burst into tears. He's always been a logical man, run by his reason, not his emotions.

"You know what you have to do now honey, we'll get you settled at me and Mary's house, send out your resume, and you'll find a nice job and get back on your feet. You can stay with us as long as you need to. You have your own room and bathroom. All the privacy you want."

I sat there in his truck watching the familiar scenery pass by through my tear-filled eyes.

"Of course, Dad. Thank you."

But it wasn't the answer I wanted.

I spent the next few weeks trying desperately to get back on my feet. For hours and hours every day, I would search job ads online, hoping to find something to give my days some meaning. If not that, stability at least. Ray was always in the back of my mind, but as the days rolled on, I came to the realization that we were going down different paths. I knew in my heart I was meant for different things; adventure, travel, purpose, yet, I had no idea where to begin.

I was lost.

I had no clue where I was meant to be. What I was destined to be doing with my life.

Then, one magical day, fate happened.

I was sitting in my dad's office searching for job opportunities in Ottawa, when I saw an ad that immediately caught my eye:

Assistant Manager needed for a small hotel in Siem Reap, Cambodia.

And underneath was a beautiful picture of a small, orange-stuccoed hotel with an open restaurant under a slate roof, surrounded by lush green palm trees, and backing onto a big pool.

It looked like a dream.

My thought, as well as anyone's I'm sure, was, *this is way too good to be true.* But that serendipitous feeling in my gut made me reply to the ad and forward my resume. Why not?

A few days later, I received an email from the owner of the hotel, Jon. He told me he was a Canadian living in Ottawa too, and co-owned The Lotus Lodge with his brother Mitch, who was living in Cambodia at the time. He was inexperienced in hospitality and was alone out there, so he needed someone to help him run their hotel. He told me that he was interested in meeting me, and I started to believe it was all real.

I met Jon a few times at a nearby coffee shop, and we got on very well. He was a young, cute guy, and showed me pictures of Mitch and The Lotus Lodge; told me all about Siem Reap, and a few of the aspects to managing the hotel. I had zero experience with management and hotels, however he seemed to look for personality over qualifications; someone okay with living in a third world country, open to adventure, and who would get along well with his brother Mitch.

"So, what makes you want to move to Cambodia? It's a pretty brave decision to make."

I smiled at Jon, then looked deep inside myself for the answer. "Well, I guess it's a feeling I have. I don't think there is anything for me here. I don't want to just live a life of routine and normality. I think, deep down, I've always felt like I was meant for something else. Something exciting. Something different perhaps. I've never been too scared to try something new, so, I just know I will be fulfilled with this new adventure!"

Jon's eyes lit up as I answered him. He seemed to understand where I was coming from.

Sometimes, you just need to let go of your past in order to move forward.

***

I never believed in fate before that day; but it was like the universe was handing me this opportunity in the palm of its hand. I had to go. No question.

Telling my old-fashioned European family the news was a whole other story. They weren't thrilled with me going to University in Toronto, four hours away, let alone travelling to the other side of the world, all by myself, to work at a hotel for an unknown amount of time. My dad took it worst. He wanted me home, with a serious job, a house, and a savings account. The yelling and fighting did almost stop me from going, but the little voice in my head kept telling me I had to. My mom, always my biggest supporter, took it best. She was devastated, don't get me wrong. But I think she knows me more than I know myself, and she knew this was meant to be.

A month after I officially got the job, February 2013, I was on a plane, with my whole life packed into one suitcase, flying to Asia. I can't begin to explain how I felt on that plane. Fear? Excitement? Wonder? Curiosity? I was overwhelmed with emotion. I kept staring out the little plane window, imagining what Cambodia, *Cambodia*, must be like.

I look back on that day all the time; the day my life really began.

Chapter 2

Cambodia

The first thing I remember when I landed in Siem Reap, was the heat. It hit me like a brick. I walked out of the plane next to palm trees dancing in the propeller's wind, feeling the hot breeze on my face, and I was overcome with excitement.

After I finished with customs, I walked outside and immediately saw Mitch waiting for me with his friend Sean. Mitch, with his little wheelchair and his huge smile.

"Hey! You must be Veronica! Welcome to Cambodia! So nice to finally meet you!"

We shook hands.

"Nice to meet you too! I am so excited to be here!" I couldn't wipe the smile off my face. I was in a different world.

We got in a local tuk-tuk, which is basically a motorbike pulling a wheeled cart; South East Asia's version of a taxi. We drove through Siem Reap while Mitch and Sean gave me a little tour.

Siem Reap was even more amazing than I fantasized. It was incomparable to any other place I had ever been. It was small, with no building more than three stories high, and jam-packed with excitement and life. The roads were dusty and had no order to them, full of honking horns and motorbikes and tuk-tuks swerving about.

I could feel the city's energy in my veins. People were selling fruit and souvenirs in street side vendors, children ran and played shoeless in the streets, expats rode around with food in their bike baskets, stray dogs hunted for food; that place was just the epitome of beautiful chaos.

They brought me to a small bamboo bar. Even the bar was exotic; fairy lights, bamboo walls, cushioned seats, and the coolest looking hippies sitting at the bar drinking beer and passing a joint around. Mitch, Sean, and I sat under the colorful lights, had one-dollar beer, and spent hours getting to know each other.

"So, what brought you two to Siem Reap of all places?" I asked as I sipped my vodka soda.

"Well, long story!" laughed Sean. "Quite spontaneous actually. Mitch and I were traveling around Cambodia a couple of years back, just checking out the sights and doing some filming for fun. We loved the place right away. And when Mitch saw The Lotus Lodge, he and his brother bought it without thinking twice."

"Yeah man," Mitch exclaimed, "sometimes you just have to listen when fate calls you, you know?"

I smiled. "Yes, I completely understand."

"How do you feel about Siem Reap so far?" asked Sean.

"I love it! It's so lively and exciting...so exotic! I can't wait to do some more exploring."

"Careful...once the travel bug bites, you can never get rid of it."

Mitch and Sean were inspiring to me; they seemed to have been everywhere. They hitch-hiked around South

America, motorbiked around Asia, been on numerous adventures; I felt like I had never really lived compared to them. I wished for experiences like theirs; little did I know I would get that wish, and then some.

***

My first day at The Lotus Lodge was an exciting one; it was even more beautiful than the pictures. Mitch showed me around, from the huge garden filled driveway out front, to the poolside restaurant out back. The staff, who were all local Cambodians, were the kindest people I had ever met.

"Hello! My name is Veronica! I am here to help Mitch run The Lotus Lodge. So nice to meet you!"

Lyda and Nareth shook my hand with big smiles on their faces. Two gorgeous young ladies who radiated softness and sincerity.

"Welcome Vee! First time to come to Cambodia?"

"Yes! I love it so far!"

"We can't wait to show you life in our country!"

We all became instant friends, and later on, almost like family.

The next few days I took time to learn not just about the ways of the hotel and what my responsibilities were, but also the ways of Cambodian life. It was slow! I was so used to the Western way; go, go, go! In Cambodia, time almost doesn't exist. Things start when they want, finish when they want. People lived slowly, enjoying the day for what it was, not staring at their watches and running off to the next meeting. I was hooked instantly.

Some hotel staff members eventually took me out to some various Cambodian activities on my days off, to proudly show me their culture and lifestyle.

One of the first day trips we did was to Kulen Mountain. Kulen Mountain is just that, a small mountain, but also covered in thick jungle; I had never seen the jungle before! The noises, the smells, the sights of the twisty trees and hanging vines; I felt like I was Jane in *Tarzan*. We drove our motorbikes down bumpy roads through the towering trees, until we got to, what I assumed was a parking lot. It was dusty and hot, and we parked our bikes and began to walk down a grubby path through the jungle.

"Where are we going, you guys?"

"We show you beautiful waterfall, Vee."

And that is just what they did.

We arrived in a massive opening in the jungle, where there was an enormous waterfall cascading down a rocky cliff into a huge pond. I was awe stricken. Suddenly, everyone took off their jackets and shoes and jumped into the water.

"Come in, Vee!"

"Um, are there leeches?"

"What are leeches?"

"Screw it, never mind, coming in!"

I spent all day swimming and splashing around in that cold water, enclosed by the jungle, with my new friends.

Later, the hotel staff brought me to the countryside for one of their 'barbecues.' Even Mitch told me it was worth going to see. Who doesn't love barbecues, right?

We all crammed into a couple of tuk-tuks, everyone with a few pots and pans on their laps, and we drove out to see Cambodian countryside. As we drove along those dusty, bumpy roads, I got a glimpse of local life. Villagers lived in homes built out of wood or bamboo, up on tall stilts (which I later learned was to keep their homes from flooding during the monsoon season). Their property was covered in lime green rice fields, which was how they either fed themselves, or made money. Even though I did believe that was what poverty looks like, I had never seen happier people. Men were pulling ox carts through the fields, waving at us as we drove by, women, wrapped in colorful scarves, peeled vegetables, or dried out the rice on straw mats in the sun, and children ran around playing and laughing with sticks or ratty toys. They lived so simply yet were more content than the richest people I knew.

We stopped our tuk-tuks in the middle of a dusty road, surrounded by muddy fields.

"We here now, Vee," shouted Rotha happily.

I looked around confused.

"Where is here?"

Everyone got out and began setting up what their version of a barbecue was. They found a nice shady place under a tree and began digging a big hole. They then stuck a few sticks along the top of the hole and lit a fire underneath it; a homemade barbecue right in the ground. Amazing.

The women put some water in a pot and began boiling rice; the only food they actually brought with them. All of a sudden, I saw the men take off their shirts and shoes and jump into the muddy, waist deep rice field water. They dunked their heads in, fishing about, came out holding God knows what, and threw them on the road.

That's when I realized they were throwing living creatures; everything from slugs and frogs, to little fish and beetles. The women then ran around with their flip flops in their hands, chasing the jumping little critters, and smashed them with their shoes! When they were dead, they placed them on the barbecue to cook.

I sat there watching in utter amazement. I'm pretty sure my jaw was hanging open. No grocery store, no market, just fresh food right out of the wild.

"Vee, want to try?"

"Yes, I will try the fish and snails please!"

We barbecued all the insects and fish, and ate lunch while sitting under the tree chatting away and playing cards. That was the day I tried my first beetle! Living in the moment of the amazing experiences that were happening all around me, I couldn't say no. Tasted quite crispy and salty; I'd go so far as to even compare it to a potato chip. Well that's what I told myself it tasted like at least.

It's amazing how wide your comfort circle grows through each new experience. It was a day I'll always remember.

Some people live grilling fresh salmon in their backyard listening to classic rock on their expensive stereo, while their kids splash around in the pool and their friends mix fresh margaritas on the patio. All the while, other people live hunting bare foot in the mud for anything living that can feed their family. The cruelty or blessing of chance is the only certainty we know. I spent my childhood summers playing at our lakeside cottage with my brother Joey, while these astounding people grew up searching for their own food and herding oxen around the sun-scorching fields, all because fate drew us those cards.

***

For Mitch and I, The Lotus Lodge wasn't just our home, it was our whole life. It kept us busy, from the moment we first opened our eyes in the morning, until our last minute of the day. There was always something, whether it be groceries needed for the kitchen, or an accidental overbooking. Maybe one of the air-conditioning machines in a guest room was broken, or the pool was beginning to look green. It never ended.

Neither one of us had any real management training, we just worked together to do our best to keep it running. We learned as we went along. Lessons were thrown at us every day.

We just took it one day at a time.

Problems had to be tackled as they came, and we relied on the staff's faithfulness to help us when things got tough. In high season, we rushed around day and night to keep our guests content and the hotel cleaned and stocked up. In low season we worked together cutting costs and budgeting the small income the hotel brought in. It was a challenge, but one I happily welcomed.

One morning, I was sitting at the computer in the office, just sipping some tea and answering emails. The office was at the front of the hotel, and the window looked out into the wide-open front lot. From the corner of my eye, I noticed a big and grey animal walking past the window.

Then another one.

It took a few seconds for me to register that they were water buffalo.

Hold on a second, they shouldn't be walking around our hotel, should they?

It's quite normal for water buffalo to wander the dusty roads of Cambodia. However, they usually didn't get past our front gates.

I ran outside and saw the pack head behind the main building toward the restaurant and pool area.

Oh no.

I rushed after them, and came upon a restaurant full of shocked-faced guests, staring at the massive water buffalo leisurely walking around our pool. Their gigantic front horns poking at the flower pots they were sniffing.

What do I do?

"Umm, don't worry folks! They're not dangerous!" *I don't think so anyway.* "Just continue eating your breakfast!"

Guests snickered and murmured as I tried to figure out what to do. I slowly walked toward the beasts, and waved my arms up and down, hoping to scare them away. But they just glanced up at me, then continued to sniff at our flowers, moving from pot to pot. Exploring their new grazing ground.

"Uh, buffalo! Leave!" I tried to scare them again.

They didn't even budge.

I was way too scared to go any closer.

Guests giggled a bit louder. I heard cameras. My face turned red.

One of the waitresses rushed off to the front of the hotel, and grabbed a tuk-tuk driver. He hurried over to me, laughing. "Don't worry, Vee. Go stand over there." He then turned toward the buffalo, and shouted, "HA! HA! GO! GO!" at the top of his lungs, before running toward them! They looked up and then scampered out of the pool area, and back out the gates, where he was so expertly herding them.

I stood there in amazement. I was amused, but also embarrassed.

The guests still stared on. Some had video cameras out recording the whole incident.

"Um, well, glad that's taken care of! Okay everyone, enjoy the rest of your day!" I shouted as I attempted to confidently walk back to the office.

Just another typical day at The Lotus Lodge.

***

But on the other side of things, the hotel was also our paradise. I was constantly surrounded by exotic animal noises, the sounds of monks chanting in the distance, and happy guests laughing in the pool. Mitch and I made it feel comfortable and inclusive to everyone staying in our sixty-person guesthouse. We held parties every few weeks, with free drinks, live music, and contests; not thinking about profit, but more so to bring everyone in town together, guests and expats alike. We held yoga classes sometimes, or book clubs. We designed our own menu, trying out different dishes, and always made the time to get to know all our guests; even taking them out occasionally.

We had dreams for that place. And although it eventually ended, for those couple of years I was home.

"Morning, how's it going?" Mitch wheeled into the staff room with his favorite coffee. I was sitting in my seat at the computer, adding bookings to our calendar, which was one of my responsibilities.

"Yeah it's good! Got three new bookings for tomorrow, so I think we're going to have a busy weekend."

"Awesome. So, what do you think about the pool area? We should fix it up a bit. Give it some color." One thing I learned about working with Mitch was he loved having guests hanging out at our hotel; so we were always all about jazzing up the place.

"Yeah good idea," I took a sip of my tea. "What do you want to do? Go buy more flower pots like last week?"

"I was thinking about hanging up a few lights in the poolside trees. Make it cozier at night time. What do you think?"

"Yeah man, sounds good! I'm ready when you are."

We got into our tuk-tuk, and headed to town to visit a small light store. We spent a few minutes browsing around looking for pretty fairy lights, when I saw him. Cory was the polar opposite of Ray in every way possible. He was tall with tattoos, light hair, and looked like a guy without a care in the world.

"Hey. Are you American?"

He had the thickest English accent I had ever heard.

"Oh my gosh no! I'm Canadian actually!" he laughed.

"Oops sorry! Canadian! I was trying to guess the accent."

"Where are you from?"

"A small town just outside of London. Are you new in Siem Reap? I haven't seen you around before."

I blushed. "Yes, I've only been here a couple of weeks actually. Just started working at The Lotus Lodge with my friend Mitch over there. I love it so far! What about you?"

"I've been living here for a couple of years actually."

"Wow! Well that means it must be a good place to live then."

"Yes, it's the best! Well, if you're new around here, how about I show you around some time? There are tons of great cafés and bars worth getting to know."

I tried so hard to come off as nonchalant.

"Yes. That would be nice actually."

He took out a pen and some paper from his pocket and handed it to me.

"Well, if you're okay with it, why don't you write down your number and I'll give you a call sometime."

Well that was the first time a charming Englishman ever hit on me, so I obviously scribbled down just that.

"Sounds great. I look forward to it."

He gave me a cute half smile as he walked out of the shop.

Mitch couldn't refrain from playfully mocking me the whole drive home.

We did meet up a few days later, at his friend's bar. I thought he looked so cool, and dangerous, and exciting. We talked and joked around all night, and he brought me to a bar rooftop for a full view of Siem Reap; the city that truly never slept. Bars played music literally all night; some places didn't close until after sunrise. Expats and locals alike strode up and down the streets, going from bar to bar, laughing, drinking, with not one worry in their minds. There was an unexplainable energy in that city, one that made me feel truly alive.

Up there, under the bright star lit sky is where Cory and I shared our first kiss.

He then brought me to the bar where he managed and DJed some nights, and we shared some more laughs and more drinks.

And to make him even more cool and exciting, he drove a motorbike.

Later on, we drove back to my room at the hotel, and he stayed the night. Incredibly unlike me, but I was in another world now. I was confident, exciting, adventurous Veronica now. And this Veronica will have sex on the first date!

We continued to casually see each other, falling for each other slowly, day at a time, and he became a huge part of Cambodia to me.

A few months passed, and I started a bit of a wild phase.

I can't begin to express the feeling of going from a cocooned, harnessed soul, to an independent, free spirit. Siem Reap opened up a whole new world to me, a world of care-free wild inhibitions. Where you could be what you wanted. Do what you wanted. Date who you wanted.

I felt like my barriers had fallen over. Like I was freed from a cage.

Eventually, I met some incredible girlfriends. Girls just like me. My girls. Girls who escaped the mundane pre empted cages of Western society. Girls who wanted to find purpose and joy and adventure. Girls who were raw and open with their feelings. Girls who pushed me and inspired me and helped me grow into the confident women I am today. Girls from all corners of the Earth. My girls. My Cambodian family.

They know who they are.

We were young, pretty, healthy, full of energy, and felt invincible. After work, we would ride our bikes and meet up somewhere; whether it be a hotel pool to tan and swim all afternoon or a late-night bar to dance and drink all evening. Sometimes, we rode our bikes out to Angkor Wat and other temples to explore the majestic Cambodian countryside. Other times, we danced on tables all night in the clubs, wearing neon vests and no shoes. Sometimes we went to Cory's bar to dance to his DJing. Other times we sat in cafés sipping lattes and talking about life.

Sofia, one of my best friends there and also a fellow expat, and I would often bike home together after a long night out. Me biking; her sitting on my handle bars.

"To the left! Whoa, careful! Okay, to the right!" She would playfully shout as she sat balancing on my wobbly bicycle, giving me directions.

"I got this!" I would laugh behind her. I could barely see anything with her golden hair blowing in my face. Those early mornings were our favorites; the sun was just rising, morning temple bells were ringing, the streets were at their quietest and the weather at its coolest.

It was just us. Free. Friends. Enjoying our days and not caring about anything else.

I couldn't help it. Life felt like a drug to me. I felt like I had never lived before, and now I was trying to soak up every moment, every experience, every minute of pure, wild joy I could find. If there was a party, I'd go. If there was a pool day planned, I'd be there with my bikini and tanning oil. If someone was planning a day trip to visit a few temples, count me in. If someone had drugs, well, I would try some.

I believe every girl needs a wild phase in her life, and damn, that was mine.

Even Cory and I were young, wild, and free together. It was like we were always at the highest emotion with each other; we were either drop-everything-can't-get-enough-of-you in love with each other, or we were crying and screaming and arguing like it was the end of the world.

I felt like I was living life at a million miles an hour, not thinking any further than the moment I was living in right then.

It was the best time of my life.

***

A couple of years passed, and I slowed down a bit. Even Cory and I slowed down a bit; we had less 'bouncing around on the rooftops until 5 am' nights, and more 'talking about life at the bar and then going home for a movie in bed' nights.

Slowly, the girls began to leave. To go off on their next adventures and follow their own journeys. That was the reality of expat life; nothing was forever. Everyone came and went. Goodbyes were a part of everyday life. However, Siem Reap was never the same without them.

But I still had Mitch. And Cory.

Even the Lotus Lodge ended for me. Jon and Mitch decided to sell it; however, I was not remotely ready to leave Siem Reap yet. I was at a crossroads; I could do the responsible thing and go home to Canada and start over again, or I could stay in this magical place and continue down this path of excitement filled days and star filled nights. I decided to stay. It was not a tough choice; I had to see where I would end up. What adventure life had in store for me next.

Sometimes you just know, deep in your soul, that you are on the right path.

I found a job assistant teaching at a nice international school, and then I moved into a little bachelor apartment in town; down the street from Cory, and next door to Mitch. Mitch began his own little business, and Cory opened his own English café. Life became a bit slower, easier, and for me then, nicer. There was more comfort, more early nights, and more appreciation of the real Cambodia. I even started to travel more often.

One day I was going for a nice bike ride on my day off, and I spotted an old woman. She was sitting on the side of a dusty road, and she was incredibly gaunt and skinny, with holes in her shoes and rips in her clothes. I felt for her immediately. I smiled as I biked past and stopped at the first food vendor I saw to buy some egg fried rice.

"Hello. How are you? Are you hungry?"

I passed her the food.

She smiled up at me, the brightest most genuine smile, and slowly reached for the food. She began to eat it hungrily, and then looked at me suddenly; almost embarrassed. Then something shocking happened; she offered me some. She was so hungry, so poor, so alone, with nothing to offer. But she still wanted to give me some of her food, even though it was clear that she was the one who needed it more.

I felt completely heartened. Smiling, I said no thank you, and biked off to buy her some water and more snacks.

The most generous people in the world aren't those who give a lot, but those who give everything they have, even if it's barely anything at all.

She inspired me. Moments like those alter your soul a little bit; they change your perception and transform the way you see the world. They reawaken your faith in people.

I was determined to see more of Asia and experience more moments like that one.

Chapter 3

Vietnam

One of my very first solo trips was to Vietnam; and to this day, one of my favorite countries. One of my girlfriends in Cambodia, Kate, moved to Hanoi, and I decided to go visit her. I spent a few days sightseeing the beautiful city and learning a bit more about Vietnamese culture.

Kate is someone who, to this day, inspires me to keep going. She had been travelling and living abroad a few years longer than myself, and had visited more countries than I ever dreamed of going to. I felt like she must have seen everything. A fellow North American like me, she also longed for faraway places, and felt a need to step her feet on foreign lands. I understood her, and she understood me.

It was great to catch up again and see her new home.

Generally, most of South East Asia has a similar way of life; slow paced, living off the land, and family being greatly important. Without the young strong generation working in the fields, they wouldn't eat. Without the older generation, they wouldn't have anyone to care for the children. Just like Cambodia, some older Vietnamese children would go off to the big city to work and send money home so that their younger siblings could go to school. They hoped school would give them greater opportunities in life, and greater opportunities for their families; but often a new pregnancy, or a sick elder would send them back to their homelands to work the fields again.

Poverty is truly a tough cycle to escape from.

I much prefer nature to cities, so I decided to take a bus to a small, rural village in the mountains nearby, called Mai Chau. Mai Chau is incredibly gorgeous; I was blown away by the picturesque farmlands, rice terraces, and the rolling green hills surrounding the villages.

I stayed on a homestay, which is basically a backpacker's version of a bed and breakfast. The family I was staying with lived in a small, wooden farmhouse, and I slept upstairs under a mosquito net with a full view of their barnyard and fields.

The countryside in that part of the world was like nothing I had ever seen before; it felt a world away from Canada's endless prairies and snow-capped mountain ranges.

One day, after the family cooked some local breakfast for me (basically boiled eggs with rice soup), I went on a little bike tour. The guide was the oldest son of the family I was staying with, named Hon, and we biked through the winding streets, across lime-green fields, and past quaint farms and livestock.

Halfway through our bike ride, Hon told me he needed to go buy medicine for his brother, so he left me at his friends' farm to wait for him. I thought it was strange, but I figured it might be a nice way to experience truer Vietnamese farm life.

I was sitting at a table next to their barn, looking out at the wheat field in the valley, when some of the family members approached me.

"Hello! My name is Cai, what is your name?" the lovely, I'm assuming granddaughter, asked me.

"Veronica. Nice to meet you!"

A few young men joined us at the table, and a couple of older women and a few very young children. They all gazed at me with wonder, as if I was an alien from outer space.

"Hello, I am Veronica, what's your name?" I asked the man I assumed was Cai's brother. He just smiled at me with blank eyes.

"He cannot speak English, sorry. Just me."

Cai then spoke to the other family members in Vietnamese, probably explaining my presence.

"They all want to know, where are you from?"

"I am from Canada."

I think 'Canada' was a familiar word, because that drew gasps and smiles from everyone else.

"Thank you for having me in your home, Cai."

"You are welcome."

I then noticed a figure far off in the valley, slouched over, whacking a hoe at the wheat crops. She dropped her hoe and slowly began walking over to us, and as she came closer, I noticed this woman must have been a hundred years old, at least. Her back was completely hunched over, she had a few gray locks of hair hanging low down her shoulders, and she had no teeth minus two completely black ones. But she had a sparkle in her eye, and she stared at me with the biggest smile on her face.

Oh, what that women must have seen in her life.

She suddenly began shouting at everyone angrily in Vietnamese, and they all rushed up, running in and out of the house, and bringing a large pot of tea and cups to the table. Cai began pouring me a cup. The matriarchal grandmother it seemed.

"My grandmother wants to know if you want food or drink?"

"This tea is just perfect Cai. Please tell her I say thank you!"

The grandmother kept talking to Cai and smiling right at me. She seemed to have such depth to her, I wish I could have spoken with her directly.

"Grandmother says you are very beautiful. And she tells you to drink her special tea."

With that, Cai grabbed another small pot and poured me a shot glass sized cup of tea. I happily took it. But before I took a sip, she said to me, "She says it is her secret tea. She makes herself. She says it will make you live forever."

Well, looking at Grandmother, I believed her!

"Well, tell her I say thank you very much."

With that, I took a gulp. I can only describe the taste as pure Earth; soil, roots, manure, who knows what. Not the yummiest tea, but if it makes you live forever, pass me more!

"Very Good!" I said as I slowly sipped another small glass.

A while later, Hon came back. I said goodbye to the lovely family, and we headed back out on our bikes. We continued further through stunning countryside, when we slowed down and pulled over next to a small wooden house.

"One moment," he said quickly.

Suddenly, a young man rushed out of the house, and ran up to Hon, who then pulled out a round, black pouch of something from his jacket pocket, snuck it to the young man, who then quickly took off. I followed him feeling a bit dismayed, and when I looked back, the young man had already disappeared back into his house.

"My brother's medicine," he explained calmly as we continued biking.

I didn't say a word.

I guess in Vietnam, there are other ways to leave the cycle of poverty; selling heroin.

***

A few days later, I headed to the famous Halong Bay, which is a warm, deep blue bay home to dozens of tall, rocky islands. It's well known for its boat trips; where you can cruise around the islands for a couple of days, spending all your time fishing, sun tanning, and kayaking around the coves. I had never seen anything quite like it before in my life.

I stayed on a nice boat for two nights, and was, oddly enough, accompanied by a few other Canadians. They were travelling around Asia for six weeks, and of course, we came to be companions during our time on the boat. We ate all our meals together, kayaked in pairs, and even bravely jumped off the boat's roof and swam to secluded beaches to spend the afternoons.

"What do you guys miss the most from home?"

"Hmmm, probably my favorite coffee place, or those maple syrup cookies I love."

41

"Oh yeah, I miss those too!" I exclaimed, as we sat there in the sand soaking up the hot, Vietnamese sun.

"Veronica, you've been away so much longer than us, do you ever get homesick?"

It's an interesting question; one I've heard quite often. And I always find it so hard to answer.

"Well, I miss my parents. And my brother. But no, not really. Right now, this feels like home. Yesterday, Kate's apartment in Hanoi felt like home. A week before that, Siem Reap was my home. I'm just too excited to find out where my next home will be."

Some people understand that feeling. Some don't.

***

I eventually headed south, stopping in one of my favorite little cities, Hoi An.

I arrived early in the morning, and took a taxi from the airport right to my hotel to check in. I was on quite a budget, so I stayed in a place that only cost me fifteen dollars a night. What a steal. Unfortunately, 'cheap hotels' in South East Asia can usually be affiliated with 'run down', 'filthy', and even 'unsafe'. My windowless room had one small bed with sheets that looked like they had never been cleaned, a rusty bathroom with only a trickle of water, and the toilet was dark a hole in the floor.

And I hate to say it, that wasn't the worst place I had ever stayed.

At that point, the only worry floating through my mind was safety, when my eyes were immediately drawn to the broken lock on the door, and the sounds of shouts and thumps from rooms all around me. Like most places I stayed before that one, I never trusted locks anyways.

Travelling alone does make you a bit paranoid at times.

I spent my nights there half asleep, listening to the sounds of people walking around the hallways, shouts from the street below, and of course, a dresser pushed up against the door.

Whatever I could do to feel safe.

As a traveler, you are constantly bombarded with stories of robberies, break-ins, and horror stories of being a girl on her own. You begin to make up rules for yourself to follow at all times: 1) Make sure someone always knows where you are going. 2) Never let random strangers know you are travelling alone. Say you are "meeting your friends" later or something along those lines, if they do ask if you are alone. Which they always do. 3) Do not keep credit cards or passports in your purse. Those basically have a big bullseye on them. 4) Trust your gut.

As paranoid as those rules make me sound, I followed them closely for many years. And they saved me on more than one occasion.

As I began to fall asleep, I drowned out the noise of people outside, and the fears of one of them breaking into my room, and dreamed of the beautiful exploring I would get to do over the next few days.

I found there was always a wonderful balance with travel; the uncomfortable risks and fears balanced with the eye-opening new experiences and unforgettably wonderful memories. It was what life really is all about.

***

Hoi An was a small, coastal town, with an old Vietnam feel. But to me, it was just dreamy. The buildings were all small, stone structures, covered in flowers and climbing vines. Red lamps hung above my head along the walking districts, strung together by yellow ribbons. There was a river running through the little city, covered in romantic foot bridges and floating candles sparkling on the water. And, as I walked down the streets, I could hear classical music coming from all the speakers attached to the lamp posts.

As I wandered the sidewalks in pure bliss, listening to Mozart playing in the air, I honestly couldn't believe that place really existed.

Just like Siem Reap, there was a huge fresh food market. It was covered by tarp to protect you from the sun, and once you enter, it's hard not to get lost in the maze-like alleys. I bought bags full of fresh mangos, bananas, and lychees, all for about two Canadian dollars.

Most of the sellers were woman, smiling at you, hoping desperately that you will buy food from their stall. Their husbands and sons were all back on the farm, picking fruit and vegetables for tomorrows merchandise. Some of the women even had small babies attached to their hips. I swear I saw a few as young as newborn. Nurseries, nannies, and babysitters are luxuries we definitely take for granted.

"Hello miss! Would you like some good fruit? I have fresh fruit just for you!"

"Miss, miss! My fruit is the best fruit!"

"Come here miss, my fruit is the most fresh!"

It was overwhelming.

"Hello," I heard the softest voice speak in my direction. I turned around to see a beautiful young woman; she couldn't have been older than twenty and was at least nine months pregnant. And the crazier part was she had two small children sitting next to her.

"Hello," I walked toward her stall, admiring the reds, yellows, and greens from her produce.

"Would you like something? I give you good price."

"Yes, actually, I would love some mangos. Maybe some lychees and bananas too?"

She smiled and filled a bag for me.

"Is this fruit from your home?" I asked.

"Yes. My village. All fresh."

"Wow. You must live in a beautiful village."

"Yes. Very nice. My mother and father stay at my home. They grow the food fresh for my shop. My husband is a farmer too."

I smiled at her and gave her an extra tip.

At least three generations all under one roof sounds like a nightmare to me, but it's the way of life out here. And necessary for survival.

I ended Vietnam in the south, in the famous Ho Chi Minh City. It was like a bigger, crazier version of Siem Reap! Crossing the roads in that city is a life-or-death situation; you dodged one car or motorbike, while you waited for another to whiz right by you. It became a skill I slowly mastered.

More traffic. More noise. More people. More chaos.

I was in love.

I met Cory there for his holiday, and we got on a motorbike and drove along the coast to his favorite city, Mui

Ne. It was a very small fishing town, with the relaxed vibe of a beach town, and the friendly locals of a village. The two of us blissfully spent the week swimming, eating fresh seafood, and motorbiking around the famous sand dunes; a little glimpse into the mystical beauty of what the desert must look like.

Cory and I were sitting in a small coffee shop one afternoon, sipping on the strongest coffee I had ever tasted.

"One day, I want to buy a motorcycle down here, and drive all the way across Vietnam, up into Laos. Maybe even Thailand. Hell, I'll even keep going up into China. I would love to do that. You should even come, Veronica; it'll be just me, you, and my motorbike."

I took another sip of my coffee.

We were sitting outside on a patio next to the water. The ocean waves crashed against the shore, and the air smelled like fresh fish.

"That sounds amazing, Cory," I smiled. "Maybe one day soon!"

Cory was so much like me; someone who dreamed of freedom and adventure. And maybe that was our problem.

When two wild people fall for each other, it's hard to find stability. We all need someone to keep us sensible and grounded. Someone to bring us down from the clouds. But when you're both dreamers, both wildly adventurous, there's no one there to keep you from flying too high. You both want to keep going. You both continue living life in the fast lane and never worry about when to exit. You feed off each other's energy. But there's no way you could be without each other, for the two of you are the only home you have; the only constant and comfort; the only safety net.

Two people with wild souls are both impossible to be with, and impossible to be without.

Chapter 4

Laos

Another one of the first trips I ever took by myself was to Laos. I knew so little about that country, besides it being next to Vietnam, which made me beyond curious to visit it.

I flew into Luang Prabang, one of Laos' quiet cities in the north. Also, one I'd heard amazing things about from friends who had been there before. Luang Prabang could be described as complete, utter peace. I felt like I had to tip toe around the city, so as not to disturb the air. Similar to other South East Asian cities, but at that time, far less touristy. At sunrise every day, hundreds of orange cloak-clad monks would walk the streets to the city center temple. I remember how amazed I was when I saw my first monk—so exotic and mysterious—but in Laos, it was a daily occurrence; it quickly became the norm.

I spent a few days exploring the pristine Kuang Si waterfalls, before I took what I thought would be an event free bus ride south.

I chose to take a VIP tourist bus to Vang Vieng, backpackers paradise according to a few friends, because I wanted something safe and fast. The bus was almost the size of a double decker, with large, reclining seats and huge windows to watch the scenery go by. *Perfect*, I thought.

What I didn't know prior to that trip was that almost the entire road to Vang Vieng was along a very steep cliff. I also forgot that I was in South East Asia, and that safety procedures and standards don't quite exist like they do back home.

Not only was the whole route along a cliffside, sans safety fence might I add, but it was also incredibly twisty and winding. So, as we drove along, the tall bus would just barely make the turns, leaning over the cliff as it did. Wobble, wobble. Back and forth. I chose a window seat of course, which unfortunately gave me a full view of the cliffs below us. Scarier still, there were actual cars and buses crashed at the bottom of some cliffs! I felt nauseous and kept planning my emergency escape strategy in my head. This lasted for over five hours.

I almost kissed the ground when we finally arrived.

***

I had heard that Vang Vieng was a back-packer's paradise, and I was not disappointed. That is just what it was. The small, cliff enclosed town was full of life; from young families there to kayak along the river, to young post-graduates planning to let loose before their adult realities slapped them in the face.

I visited small caves, farmlands, and even kayaked down the Mekong; calmly flowing along mountain ranges and rice fields. Occasionally, I would encounter a drunk tourist floating in a tube down the river—a common touristy activity for young travelers to do in Vang Vieng. There were bars spread out all along the riverside, so people could float from bar to bar, getting drunker and drunker.

It was entertaining to see, I will admit.

Unfortunately, a few years later, some tourists died on that river, and last I heard they had to close it down. Now they are apparently digging out mountain sides, so they can build huge chain hotels to attract more high-end tourists. It's such a shame.

One day, I decided to go for a bike ride down some mountain trails. I was there all day, riding and soaring through the huge trees, fields, and valleys. I felt so free. However, sometimes experience teaches us important life lessons, and that day I learned this; never go mountain biking wearing flip flops. What an idiot I was.

As I was speedily coasting down a hill, I smashed my right foot on a boulder. A sharp pain zapped up my leg like an electric shock. When I looked down, my entire nail had lifted off my big toe.

I think it would have hurt less if I had just cut the whole toe off. I could barely scream, because I was so shocked and in such searing pain. I carefully climbed off my bike and used it as a crutch to hop myself down the mountain and to anywhere, anyone, who could help.

I was in so much pain, I was trying not to vomit.

I hopped down the road, initially planning on going back to my guesthouse, when I passed the Vang Vieng hospital. I didn't even think twice. I hobbled into the empty hospital. It was spotless and shiny and just like any small hospital you would see back home.

I couldn't see another soul.

"Hello?" I said. My voice echoed down the hallway.

No one was there.

I kept on hobbling around the hallways, until I saw a nurse's station. I peered in the doorway, and saw two young female nurses sitting on the ground playing something on their phones.

They glanced up at me.

"Can you please help me? My foot…" and I pointed down to my butchered toe and the trail of blood I was leaving behind.

They quickly got up and walked over to me, looking at what the problem was. They said something I couldn't understand, and ushered me to the emergency room. I was desperately holding in tears.

I don't know why they brought me there, this clearly wasn't an emergency. I just think it was the most convenient place for them.

"Can you help my toe? I think I ripped off the nail. Maybe it's broken, I'm not sure."

The nurses just ushered me to lay on the bed, and I realized they spoke zero English.

I clearly wasn't in an international hospital.

They shuffled around the room, grabbing supplies, then they began cleaning the blood off my foot. One nurse, out of nowhere, picked up a huge needle and shot my raw toe skin with it. I almost screamed in pain.

"What is that?"

No answer of course.

The other nurse then began carefully cutting off the dead toe nail.

Whatever that needle was, it wasn't a numbing agent.

They cleaned, poked, prodded, wrapped, and x-rayed. They even gave me a little to-go baggy full of wound cleaning products, antiseptic, fresh wraps, and painkillers.

I was impressed.

They then pointed out the door and to a desk.

The bill. *Uh oh.*

I didn't even think about paying for this, or how much it was going to cost. I'm a spoiled Canadian swimming in pools of free healthcare, and I forgot visiting foreign hospitals often meant you'd be leaving with a huge bill.

I limped over to the desk, and the man behind it looked in my bag and punched some numbers on his calculator. I began thinking to myself, *It's okay, as long as you're fine. You have your credit card with you, worst case. Plus, I have some money saved just for this type of situation. Don't worry. It'll be fine.*

He handed me over the calculator.

$6.50.

"Six dollars and fifty cents? American? Six dollars?" I held up my fingers to confirm. It couldn't be this cheap. *Maybe he meant six hundred?*

He nodded at me. Yes, six dollars and a half.

So, I passed him some coins I had in my pocket.

Wow.

I walked out of that hospital, with a clean, freshly wrapped toe, no major injuries, a huge packet of pain killers, and only six and a half bucks poorer.

I love Laos.

Chapter 5

Bali

Bali.

You hear that word back in Canada, and you think of the Garden of Eden.

And is it over-rated?

Not one little bit.

Today, I can say I've been to Bali multiple times; I literally cannot get enough. But my very first time was in 2015, and I stayed the whole summer.

Summer 2015. That'll be a tough one to top. I spent weeks exploring the island; north, south, east, west. The west was quite packed with tourists but had massive beaches and was a surfer's nirvana. The north and east had incredible black sand beaches and views of volcanos. Quite a sight to see! The south had massive cliffs, rocky beaches, and some unbelievable roads for motorbiking. An A+ for its views for sure.

But my favorite part was the middle—Ubud. Imagine a land of lush green jungle, bright green rice terraces, and untouched temples. Now sprinkle on some yoga studios, infinity pools, and vegan cafes. That was Ubud.

I know it sounds so cliché, but I truly discovered so much about myself there. I learned how comfortable and content I am on my own. I learned how I wished for a life of peace and purpose. And I learned to love yoga.

Today I call myself a vegan yogi hipster…and I blame it all on Ubud.

After a few blissful weeks of yoga in the mornings and jungle walks in the evenings, I decided I was due for a bit of adventure. I heard about a well-known trek many hikers seem to rave about; the Mount Rinjani climb over on Lombok Island.

I have always considered myself somewhat fit. I spent my whole childhood playing sports, and I've been jogging almost daily ever since high school. So, a hike on a volcano sounded like something that wouldn't be too much of a problem for me.

Let's just say I have never been less prepared for something, even today.

I booked a guide and porters for the two-night three-day hike, opposed to the other one-night two-day hike. I mean, go big or go home, right? I bought all the equipment they told me I would need; a warm jacket, water proof pants, good hiking shoes, lots of layers, and a hat and gloves. Done. No problem.

I arrived on Lombok a day before my hike started, to do a bit of exploring. Lombok was another world away from Bali; barely any tourists, not a lot of money, and all very traditionally Indonesian.

I was also lucky enough to be there for Ramadan! This gave me a bit more understanding of the holiday; It is an Islamic ritual observed by Muslims world-wide as a month of fasting. People practicing this celebration would not eat, or even drink water, any time after sunrise or before sunset.

I stayed in a homestay with a lovely young family, who of course were practicing Ramadan while I was there.

It was five o'clock that evening, and I was already feeling quite hungry. I walked into the little kitchen in their home and began looking at the menu on the wall. The wife saw me and walked over.

"Can I get you something to eat miss?" she smiled.

I was about to answer, when I noticed the sun was still out. *These people haven't eaten all day. I can't make them cook for me right now. I would feel selfish.*

"Um, you know what, I think I will wait an hour? Maybe just some tea for now."

I think she realized what I meant.

"It's okay, we are okay; I can cook for you now if you are hungry."

"It's okay, I promise, just tea is fine."

I felt like I would be completely rude if I sat there eating noodles while they watched with empty bellies.

So instead, I sat with my tea just watching all the villagers walking around the dusty streets with their baskets and carts, and school children running home in time for their sunset dinner.

I also saw the young boys who lived at the homestay standing outside on the front step, huddled together, staring at the setting sun. They looked so anxious, and so excited. Slowly, the bright orange sun dropped below the horizon, and the boys cheered and ran into the kitchen. I heard pots and pans and plates clanging together.

Dinner was finally served.

The wife walked over to me and asked, "Now that we eat, do you want to join us for dinner miss?"

"I would love to!" I happily answered.

So, I sat there on that big wooden table, a day before my hike, eating rice and vegetables with a lovely Indonesian family in Ramadan.

***

Before the sun even rose the next day, I was up, dressed, backpack on, and waiting for my drive to Mount Rinjani. I got there and met my friendly local guide, Sam, the two porters, and the two nice hikers joining me on the hike as well.

It began easy; just a steady uphill walk through some bushy fields. I remember looking up at the top of Rinjani from there, thinking, *I got this.*

"So, what brings you guys here?" I asked the couple there with me.

"Actually, we both have a little summer holiday, and thought to meet up and do some hiking! What about you?"

"Kind of the same actually."

"Where are you from?"

"Canada. Ottawa…do you know it?"

"Yes, of course I know Ottawa, I'm from Canada too!" one of them answered.

"Wow! What a small world. What about you?"

"I am from Norway," the other young woman replied. "Do you still live in Ottawa?"

"Well, no," I answered, "I actually live in Cambodia right now."

They both looked at me with wide eyes. "What? Really? That's amazing! What brought you there?"

I proceeded with trying to explain. It's always a tough one for me.

Remember when I said it was easy? Well after about three or four hours I didn't think so anymore.

The hike got steep! And not just steep, I mean I was on my hands and feet at some points. And every time I looked up and thought I saw the top, there was another ridge to climb. Then another. So many false peaks. My leg muscles were yelling at me and my feet were aching, but I felt quite good. Quite determined.

The energy was the biggest adrenaline booster. We would stop for breaks here and there, and then a long break for lunch, and there were always other groups or hikers there with us. We chatted, ate, just squatting in the grass. When you're so vulnerable, so sweaty, so real, so helpless, you just open up to people. We were all trying to conquer the same mountain, so we easily connected and bonded with each other. We were in it together.

The steep, uphill climb went on for hours, until right before sunset. I saw the top of that volcano, and a rush of confident energy flowed through me. It made me feel so proud of myself. Up to that point, it was physically the hardest thing I had ever done.

My group and I cheered each other on as we walked to the very top; the ridge of the volcano. It was much colder up there too.

Our porters set up our tents for us, and cooked us a simple rice dish for dinner.

They were the true superheroes; they hiked that volcano a few times a month, all while carrying supplies on their shoulders, and doing all the cooking and setting up.

My tent was right near the edge of the volcano, and I was literally in the clouds. The white puffs almost touched my tent. As we finished up our dinner, Sam came over to us. "Tomorrow morning, who wants to do the summit? Me and porters not go, so if you want to go, I will wake you up at two a.m."

The Rinjani summit is optional. It's the highest peak of the volcano, further up and along the ridge, and is known to be quite difficult. And even a bit dangerous. Out of the couple, one decided not to do it, the other did.

I did too.

At precisely two o'clock that morning, my guide had awoken me by smacking my tent. "Miss! Wake up! Time for you to hike! Sunrise in three hours."

"…huh? What?…yeah…okay…"

I sheepishly tied my boots, did up my jacket, grabbed my poles, and began the pitch-black hike up to the summit. It was completely dark, so one of the porters let me borrow his head light to see. I was questioning my decision at that point.

"Good luck, miss!" the porter told me as I picked up my poles.

"Thank you," I smiled.

As he walked back toward our tents, I turned around and faced the top of the mountain. I tried to picture it through the blackness of the night.

Alright, let's go.

The first thirty minutes or so were alright. The ground was a bit loose, so I had to give it more effort, but it wasn't too steep or unmanageable. Mostly just cold and windy.

Eventually, the ground got more and more ashy and covered by gravel, the incline got steeper, and the path got thinner. As I walked, if I looked to my right; cliff. You fall you die. If I looked to my left; cliff. You fall you die. A completely vertical drop. I had a small area to follow; so I always kept my eyes looking down. The ground was so loose, all completely pebbles and rocks, so every time I took two steps, I slid down one. Two more steps. Slid down one. It was so frustrating. I had to use all the strength I had to keep moving up.

As I got higher, it got colder. After about an hour or so, my face began to feel like ice. My hands were so cold I could barely feel my fingers. The wind was so strong, it was physically moving me. I had to use even more strength to keep myself from being blown over, down a cliff. I jammed my poles into the earth with every step I took. I couldn't hear anything but the wind and the sound of my breathing.

As I got even higher still, I could feel the difference in the air. My lungs were working extra hard to breathe in enough oxygen.

I tried to focus on my staggered breathing, but also trying to watch my feet and where I was stepping. I was so scared of stepping over the edge of the cliffside. I tried to grip my poles tightly, but my hands were becoming frozen. It was colder than I thought it would be.

Breath. Step. Look. Poles. Breath. Step. Rest.

I was getting tired. My muscles were shaking. My lungs were angry. My skin was cold. I kept having to take breaks, to gather my strength again. I wondered over and over if I was close yet. At one point I sat in the gravel, trying to catch my breath, and trying not to cry.

It felt as if I had been up there for hours. Was I even making any progress?

I shouldn't be up here. I thought to myself. *I'm not trained for this. I'm alone. I could get hurt. What am I doing?*

I started to miss my mom and dad.

Just then, I noticed something in the distance, way below me. It was a purple light. The sun was just starting to rise, and it turned the whole sky purple. The purple slowly turned to pink, and then to a soft orange hue. I began to see the light reflect off some clouds. All way below me. It was beautiful.

Wow was I high.

I had never been that high up before! Not outside of an airplane anyway. I was on top of the world. I actually climbed myself up there. I couldn't believe it.

I got a huge rush of adrenaline, a sense of confidence, and I kept on walking. Slowly, sturdily, I stepped one foot at a time; one step, pull, two steps, pull, three steps, pull…

I just focused on my breathing; stepped slow and steady. Eventually the sky got brighter. The ground got harder. The incline got flatter.

I remember that feeling when I stood up strait and walked around some huge boulders to get to the very top.

I.

Fucking.

Did it.

With a huge smile planted on my face, I walked around one more boulder, and there everyone was. All the other hikers who managed to do the summit. They turned to look at me and began cheering. I walked through a crowd of high fives, whistles, and pats on the back. Then they all turned again and began cheering on the next guy after me. We all laughed and clapped and cheered. It was the most amazing feeling of community.

We all succeeded. And we all felt proud.

I looked way down into that rocky volcano, above all the clouds. I felt weightless. I felt like I could do anything.

We all sat there, talking about our climb, watching the sky get brighter and brighter, feeling so gratified in ourselves. It was definitely my biggest accomplishment, up to that point at least.

Ultimately, the much-dreaded walk down had to happen, then a whole other day of hiking.

***

The second day was just as difficult as the first, but it felt worse because every single muscle in my body felt sore. We trekked steeply down to the volcano, around the lake in the center, and up to the ridge on the other side. There were no barriers, no fences or climbing ropes. You just had to trust your body. And never look down.

Even though it was difficult, it was beautiful. The lakes were as still as glass, with the mountains reflecting off the water like a mirror. As we got lower, the trees became thicker and greener, and there was more wildlife to spot.

Eventually, we came to some natural hot springs. They were small pools of green water, which came from under the earth and got heated up by the volcano. I never actually expected hot springs to be so hot! Me, the couple, and a few other hikers along the route, all got into our sports bras and underwear, and sat in those hot springs like we were at a five-star spa. It was paradise. My aching muscles felt soothed and my skin felt clean.

It was objectively well deserved.

We finally made it up to the opposite ridge by sunset. The porters set up our tents, and we all had dinner together around the fire; potatoes and rice with biscuits and tea.

"When I get back to civilization, I am taking a bubble bath and having an ice-cold beer," the Norwegian woman said.

"Oh man, I am definitely drinking an entire bottle of wine while I sit in an actual bed and watch trash TV," I joked back.

We all laughed.

It's amazing how when your body and mind are tested, and you haven't showered or eaten properly, or pooped properly for that matter, two days can feel like a month.

At sunrise the following morning, we headed back down the mountain. This day was the easiest, but our bodies were the tenderest. The trek down was through a thick jungle, passing monkeys, exotic birds, and other tired hikers. It took all day, but we finally made it.

My running shoes were almost completely torn up.

Seeing that big sign say, *Congratulations for climbing Mount Rinjani*, I wanted to jump up and down and cheer. I had never, up to that point, done anything quite so difficult.

My body was pushed. My mind was pushed. And I did it. As I got into a taxi, lugging my heavy, dirty back pack behind me, I had never felt prouder.

It was my first real hike, but not my last.

***

I got the taxi to drive me to the closest big town on the beach. *As long as there's a nice hotel, I'll go anywhere*, I thought. I splurged a little bit on a nice guesthouse next to the coast, with a room that opened up to a little garden. I had a comfortable bed, hot water, air conditioning, and a normal toilet.

I was in paradise.

After a few days of doing nothing but reading, writing, and resting, I headed to the coast to boat back to Bali island.

I waited at the marina among all the fishing boats for the one to take me to Eden again. There were quite a few other hikers there, waiting just like me. All of us proud of ourselves, but excited to get the hell back to Bali.

After an hour of waves and splashes, I stepped back onto the east coast Balinese beach, took a deep breath, and searched for a taxi. I wanted to spend my last couple of weeks there meditating and practicing yoga in Ubud. Waking up every morning to the sun rising on the rice fields, spending my afternoons reading books and sipping tea in cafes; before I had to head back to Cambodia to start working again.

I knew right then though; I would definitely be back one day.

Chapter 6
Cambodia

The first half of my life in Cambodia revolved around The Lotus Lodge. The second half revolved around my students. I began as a teacher's assistant, really just needing to make some money and pay my rent, but I began to fall in love with it. There was something so rewarding in the look in a child's face when they learn. Teaching children felt so purposeful.

I began to gain some experience and learn a bit about how to run a classroom. Eventually, I found an evening job teaching English to young teenagers.

It was the beginning of the path I would then follow in life.

They weren't just my students; they were my pals. They loved to write poetry, and play English games, and they always felt comfortable enough to tell me something funny that happened to them that day, or tell me why they were feeling sad. I made my own riddle games and puzzles to solve. We had days where we would write stories, play word games, or preform skits.

I was meant to do this. I felt it in my bones. Words and language have always been a part of my life, and now I get to share this with others.

I felt truly lucky.

The kids were inspiring to me as well. They weren't spoiled in anyway, they were Cambodian kids, with tough lives and no real privileges. Some had elderly relatives they had to help support. Some were learning English so they could get a good job one day and take care of their family. They dreamed of traveling to Disney land, visiting a beach, or even just playing on a sports team; things I always took for granted as a child.

Something so normal to one person, is a fantasy to another.

Just a few years prior, Cambodia was devastated by the Khmer Rouge. They were a communist party that ruled during the mid-1970s, whose goal was to establish a classless, communist country built on a rural, agricultural-based economy; they rejected all forms of capitalism.

To do this, they eliminated all use of money, free markets, normal schooling, personal property, foreign fashion, religion, and traditional Khmer culture. Public schools, pagodas, stores, and government buildings were shut down or turned into prisons or re-education camps. Even entertainment was restricted.

During the 1970s, hundreds of thousands of intellectuals, professionals, children, teachers, and ex-government officials were killed in a systematic campaign to remove those seen to be "not pure." In other words, if you were too educated, rich, or democratically minded, you were murdered. Only farmers and workers were needed in their world.

Thousands of people were held in prisons where they were interrogated, tortured, and executed.

It is estimated today that almost twenty-five percent of the population was killed during this time.

One of the sites where these atrocities happened was in the Killing Fields in Phnom Penh. As an expat in Cambodia, I felt it was important to visit that place to fully understand the suffering and strength of the Cambodian People.

That day will stick with me forever.

I visited the S-21 Prison, also known as the Tuol Sleng Museum of Genocide. It used to be a school, but was turned into a prison and torture chamber during the Khmer Rouge reign.

Around fourteen thousand prisoners entered that prison.

Only seven survived.

The bottom floor still had school desks and chairs left untouched. The prisoners' beds were all upstairs.

It felt eerie. I visited the museum during a solo trip to Phnom Penh, and I don't think I prepared myself for how gruesome and terrifying it really was going to be. I remember walking through the building in complete silence, with shivers running up my spine, and tears building up in my eyes. I realized how little I truly knew about the country, and about the people.

On one wall were horrific photographs of dead bodies chained to beds with pools of blood underneath them.

In another building, the walls were covered with hundreds of portraits. There were young children, skinny and starving, some with bruises, staring blankly into the camera. Some of mothers holding their babies, with a look of hopelessness in their eyes. These photographs were kept so the soldiers could prove to their Khmer Rouge leaders that their orders had been carried out.

It was horrifying.

The fields themselves left an imprint in me that I will never be able to scrub away.

There were covered pits of mass graves.

There were tree stumps where children and babies were smashed against and killed, before being buried with their parents.

It was silent. I could feel the desolation in my veins.

And I still will never be able to imagine the suffering felt by so many people.

***

Knowing a bit more about this emotional part of history, you would never guess it by looking in the faces of the local people.

They were always so cheerful. So full of life.

Every person I would pass on the street would always smile and wave to me. People's faces were full of carefree joy. Children playfully chased me on my bike. Their resilience astounded me.

The horrors of yesterday never ruined their joy in today. And their dreams for tomorrow.

That's why I love lotuses so much.

The lotus flower is a sacred flower in Cambodia. And not just because you can see them growing everywhere.

Lotuses grow in muddy water, standing tall, where they bloom into large flowers of pinks and whites. In Buddhism, the lotus flower represents fortune and self-regeneration: Rising and blooming above the darkness to achieve enlightenment.

That is exactly what Cambodian people are.

I found it extremely inspiring and befitting to get a lotus tattoo while I was living in Siem Reap; that's just how Cambodia made me feel.

Like a lotus.

***

A sorrowful modern history and a poverty stricken present, though, can sometimes lead to acts of desperation.

I became a victim of that desperation when I was first mugged.

Not that I'm trying to justify robbing anyone, theft is never okay, but my young, Western face does scream "I have money" to those with none.

One night, I was on my bike riding to meet Cory for dinner in town; not late, maybe seven in the evening. And stupidly, I had my headphones and music in my ears and my purse around my shoulder.

Not a care in the world.

I turned a corner, and out of nowhere a man on a motorbike drove past me, grabbed my purse, and just kept on driving.

I had no idea what was going on.

Since my purse was wrapped around my shoulder, I flew off my bike with it, and was dragged behind his motorbike. It took a few seconds before my purse snapped and he took off.

That was the day I came up with rule number three.

I was left disoriented, rolling and sliding on the course cement, still lost to what had just happened.

I gathered my bearings, and quickly crawled off the road before I got hit by a car.

I just got robbed. My skin was on fire. My arms were full of blood.

I began to cry.

Through my sobs, I got back on my bike and rode back to the hotel, shaking and shocked to what had actually just happened to me.

I was incredibly lucky that I didn't break any bones. Or cracked my skull on the cement.

When I arrived in my room, I jumped in the shower and tried cleaning my bloody wounds. All while still crying and shaking.

I got out of the shower and called Cory.

"Hello? Veronica where are you?"

"My…*sob*…bike…*sob*…I was mugged…*sob*…he grabbed my bag…*sob*…my arm and back…*sob*…dragged down the road…"

Cory interrupted me before I could get out a full sentence through my tears.

"What? Where are you?"

"At home."

"I'll be there in five minutes." Click.

Cory arrived so quickly; he must have driven a hundred miles an hour down those roads. He had antiseptic creams and cleaners, and he immediately began scrubbing out all the dirt mashed into my open wounds.

I was torn up all down my back, right arm, and right leg. It was brutal. I still have scars from that incident today. And the cleaning was just as brutal, although necessary.

I couldn't sleep properly for weeks. My scrapes and cuts were so deep, and so wide, I couldn't bear to have anything touch them until they scabbed over. It hurt too much.

I could pretty much only sleep on my left side.

Luckily, my wounds all scabbed up and healed beautifully.

Cory clearly did a great job.

I still have a few scars from that incident today, happily reminding me that the world isn't always such a friendly place. Also, when biking at night, keep alert!

Live and learn.

***

Cambodia was my world for over three years. It doesn't sound that long, but for me, it was a mini lifetime. Friendships, jobs, relationships, homes…so much changed over those years.

It was difficult to leave. The goodbyes broke my heart. But deep down I knew I needed to go. Siem Reap, that whole lifestyle, is addicting. It's easy to get sucked in and never leave. I knew I wanted more experience in the teaching field, I knew I needed to save a bit more money, and I felt it was time to follow another path and gain new experiences.

Truthfully, I knew I needed to do the adult thing for a little while. Or at least my version of it.

I arrived in Cambodia as a young, innocent, heartbroken girl ready to take on anything life threw at her. I was lost, but so excited. I didn't know much; I was quite naïve; but I was eager to learn. Eager to experience. Eager to try.

I left Cambodia as a young woman. I learned more about the world and so much more about who I was. I learned how to be content alone, and to trust myself. I embraced change, I grew a much thicker skin, and I felt more confident in my ability to explore and venture out into the unknown.

I believe we, as humans, are in a constant state of transformation. Each new person we meet and each new experience we face alters us; it changes the way we think, react, and observe the world. Every single human on this planet sees the world a different way; we all hold a completely different perception of it. This is not something we can change, but embrace. My perception of the world changed, and still changes today, with each new encounter, each new adventure, and each new foreign land I walk my feet on. Comfort zones grow, self-assurance strengthens, and a new awareness of reality begins to develop.

That is one thing about travel that is addicting to me; it changes you. I learned more about the world traveling than I ever did in school.

I urge every person, any age, to travel. Venture as far and wide as you can. I promise you; you will come back a changed person.

Chapter 7

Thailand

I had many small trips over those few years, from the Philippines, to Singapore, to Malaysia…but one place I feel worth mentioning is Thailand.

I have been to Thailand at least half a dozen times over the years. It's addicting. There's something about it I just cannot quite put my finger on, whether it's the nomadic energy, the pristine beaches, the fun-loving people; I always felt so free there.

One city that I can't get enough of is Bangkok. Bangkok is one of the most visited cities in the entire world, and it's easy to understand why. Anything goes. For all people. Do you want to sightsee ancient ruins and learn more about Thai culture? Bangkok's the place. Do you want to wear elephant pants and flip flops, walk around the bar filled streets holding buckets of alcohol and dance on tables until the early hours? Bangkok's the place. Do you want to stay in a luxurious five-star resort, sipping Mai Tai's, getting massages, and laying by the pool? Bangkok's the place. Or do you want to eat cheap pad thai, hook up with other backpackers, and visit ping pong shows? Fair enough. Bangkok's the place.

I think I was all those people in Bangkok at one point or another.

The first time I went to Bangkok I was alone. It was shortly after I first arrived in Asia and was still a bit new to traveling. I had a two-day stop over on my way to some islands, and I figured I would do some sightseeing. I stayed in a hostel right near the infamous Khoa San Road, and met some really interesting back packers from Australia. We went out one night for delicious street food, then hit up a few bars. All packed with tourists, of course. The energy was invigorating.

"Is this the vodka soda, or the gin tonic?" Ashley asked.

I was sitting with Ashley, Megan, and Lisa; three Australian girls who just finished school and were taking their compulsory pre-time-to-adult holiday.

"It's the vodka," replied Lisa.

I sat there sipping my bucket of god-knows-what, listening to the horrible DJ. "So, do you girls want to check out some other places soon?" There is only so much RnB I can sanely listen to.

"Yeah, I'm down when I'm finished with this drink," I heard one of them shout over the music.

We stumbled down the bustling streets, with music pumping from every which direction, and were stopped by a Thai man passing out business cards on the corner. "Ping pong?"

"What's all this about ping pong over here?" shouted drunk Ashley.

Ping pong shows are an infamous attraction for the late-night tourist. If you don't know what it is, it's basically a naked woman putting ping pong balls, and various other objects, up her you-know-what, and shooting them out like rockets. A family friendly show, clearly.

We looked at the cards.

"Oh my god, we should go."

"Ew no! That's so gross," Lisa replied.

"Come on, we're in Bangkok, I think we have to see this," stammered Megan.

When in Rome?

"Okay. Fine. Why not?"

The man led us to the little bar down a dark alley, and after we paid the entrance fee, we walked into a small, smoky bar with a stage in the middle. Techno music was playing. There were creepy guys sitting in the dark corners. Other drunk tourists laughing and spilling drinks at one table. Waitresses in the tiniest outfits I'd ever seen. I felt uncomfortable. Peer pressure is a bitch.

We sat down at one table near the stage and ordered a few more drinks. Soon enough, a naked woman staggered on stage, holding a bucket of ping pongs. She laid down on the stage, poured the ping pong balls out and just started stuffing them up herself. I was horrified yet couldn't look away. I have no clue, to this day, how she did it, but she shot them right out of her and they landed in the bucket! It was actually quite impressive.

There was nothing sexual about it. Just morbid.

I had no appetite for my drink.

I just kept wondering how this woman learned she could even do this?

The other girls seemed to lose a bit of their buzz too...we felt uncomfortable yet couldn't look away for some reason. Morbid curiosity.

"This is gross guys, let's go dancing," whined Lisa, who looked the least happy to be there.

Right then, out of nowhere, I kid you not, one of the ping pongs lost control, came flying toward us, and hit Lisa right on the shoulder.

I almost went deaf from her scream. The rest of us burst out laughing and couldn't stop all night.

"Screw this I am out of here guys!" she screamed and ran outside.

We all followed her out, and slowly made our way back to the hostel.

That was enough excitement for one day.

***

We all said goodbye the next morning, and I got on a rackety old bus, and headed down south.

The Thai islands, I think, are some of the most beautiful in the world. I have never seen beaches quite as stunning as the ones in Thailand. The sand was soft and white, the beaches were surrounded by tall, rocky islands and cliffs, palm trees hung over head; it was picturesque perfection.

I've been to a few islands there over the years, but my first was Koh Phi Phi. One I heard was popular to younger travelers, and had a fun, carefree scene. At only twenty-four years old at the time, it sounded perfect for me.

I arrived on a beach side town called Krabi, where I stayed for the night, then the following day, I got on a boat and sailed to Koh Phi Phi island.

What is it about the sea? The feeling of wandering freedom? The peaceful melody of the waves? The idea that you could sail away and never return? Anonymity? Seasides are always calmer. Slower. Easier.

One day, I promised myself, I will live next to the sea.

I sat there on the edge of the boat, with my feet dangling over the sides, feeling the warm, salty breeze in my hair, and the waves splashing my feet. What complete freedom.

When I arrived on Koh Phi Phi, it was like I couldn't take enough pictures. Fishing boats in the marina, tall palm trees hanging over the sandy beaches, fresh coconuts everywhere, reggae bars every few feet; It was overwhelmingly gorgeous.

I walked along the beach and found my hotel. Since Koh Phi Phi is a bit of a party island, I opted for a nicer hotel a bit higher up and away from the bars, so I could actually sleep at night. It cost more than I hoped, but I knew I'd regret it if I didn't splurge; I'm an early bird, so I get cranky without my good night's rest!

Lesson 246: Don't assume islands accept credit cards.

Back then, I only travelled with a bit of cash on me, usually just my money for food and fun. Hotels and transport I preferred to pay for with credit cards. I felt it was safer.

"Hello! I'm here to check in. Name is under Veronica."

The pretty woman in her flowing white dress looked up at me and smiled. "Hello, Miss Veronica! Welcome!"

We both had to speak loudly enough to hear each other over the sounds of waves crashing below.

"I see you're in a double room, ocean view. Four nights?"

"Yes! That's perfect, thank you. Can I please pay now?"

I handed over my credit card. Even to this day, I love to pre-pay for things while travelling, it helps me budget.

She looked solemnly at the credit card.

"Oh, I'm sorry miss, we don't have a credit card machine here. We only accept cash."

"What? Really?" I expected a nice place like that would surely accept credit cards.

"I'm so sorry, there are ATMs on the island though."

"Oh, that's good then." I looked through my wallet. "Oh, actually I think I have just enough in cash. I can to go the ATM later for more money."

"Great!"

So, I paid her in cash. Almost all of my money.

I spent the whole day in paradise. I jumped on a fishing boat and went island hopping most of the afternoon; coasting through the waves to see nearby beaches and completely remote islands.

Back on Phi Phi, I walked up the beach a bit, found a cool café playing some Bob Marley, and sat on a beanie chair in the sand with my book and a cold beer. *I'm never leaving*, I thought to myself.

Later on, I ordered an early dinner, and after I paid for it, I realized I was almost completely out of cash. So, I got up and went hunting for those ATMs.

I found one among all the busy restaurants, and when I slid in my card and entered my PIN, a weird message popped up on the screen: *Invalid Card. Not able to process card.* And it shot back out.

That's weird.

So, I kept walking and found another ATM. *Invalid Card. Not able to process card.*

And another ATM. *Invalid Card. Not able to process card.*

What the hell was going on?

I ran back to my hotel room and video-called my bank back in Canada; the emergency number for credit card problems. When they answered, I explained where I was and what was happening, worried that my card was blocked or something.

"Well Ms. Trunzo, everything seems perfectly fine on this end. Your card is working normally, nothing is blocked, I even made a note that you are travelling and trying to withdraw cash. Perhaps your card is damaged?"

"No, not at all, it's perfectly fine! Is this normal?"

"I'm not sure Ms. Trunzo, I haven't heard of this happening before. Why don't you go try one more time, and call back if there are any issues?"

So, I ran back to the main walking area, and tried at another ATM. *Invalid Card. Not able to process card.*

Oh my God, what's going on?

And it wasn't the ATMs, I saw plenty of other people using them with no problems. I ran up and down the bar-filled streets, starting to worry at that point, and was hoping to find a bank.

Nope.

Of course.

I found a currency exchange. Maybe they will take my credit card and withdraw it themselves? But they didn't do that. Cash only.

Oh no.

I had no money to eat the next day. I had no money to get a boat back to the main land where they had banks. Or Western Unions.

What could I do?

I ran back to my hotel and called my bank back. They tried to help, but there was nothing they could do. They said it must have been the machines, not my card.

It was getting dark. I had no money.

I headed back to the streets and wandered some more, trying every ATM I could find. The island was getting busy with tourists laughing, drinking, bar-hopping; not a care in the world. Their carefree joy emphasized by my overbearing sense of worry.

I should have just stayed in a cheap hostel and kept all my cash!

No hotels accepted credit cards either. I thought maybe I could find a hotel, pay them with my card, and they could give me cash back. Maybe they would do it if I begged hard enough.

But there were no credit card machines anywhere!

I was losing hope, ready to beg some other tourists for cash, when I saw a sign from angels; it was a hospital, but with a *VISA* sign out front. A miracle!

I rushed into that tiny hospital so quickly, breathing heavily, on the verge of tears.

The staff shot their heads up at me.

I desperately explained my situation and begged them to let me use their machine for cash back. Pretty please?

The manager seemed to feel sympathy for me and agreed, but they would need to charge a 15% commission to cover the fees.

At that point I would have paid 100% commission!

He swiped my card, and we waited.

Invalid Card. Not able to process card.

I almost burst into tears.

"Wait, let's try one more time," he turned the machine off and on again. "Okay, let's ask Buddha for good luck!"

And I did.

He swiped my card again, and we waited.

Approved.

Thank you, Buddha!

I almost jumped up and down cheering. Thank God! The other nurses were smiling, clearly seeing how relieved I was.

I took my cash and ran out of there, with a huge smile on my face.

I walked into a beach side bar, ordered a well-deserved ice-cold beer, and sat outside in the sand watching the fire dancers on the beach. My mind and body began to feel at ease again.

I made a mental note right then, *when you get back to Canada, get a new credit card.*

***

Most tourists travel to Thailand for the beaches. But one of the most under rated, under visited, and overly amazing places, is Thailand's north.

Pai is a small village way up in the mountains, surrounded by coffee plantations and rolling hills and valleys. It is a nightmare to get to though; the winding and swerving road trip, up and down mountains and around cliffs, will get anyone car sick. But totally worth it.

I had the most incredible and relaxing time; I rode my bike from coffee shop to coffee shop, visited hot springs, sat in a hammock next to the river with my book. Exploring. Eating good. Doing yoga. It would be easy to stay forever.

It was my kind of place.

But the best thing about Pai for me, is that it got me hooked on writing.

I was at a little café one afternoon; one of those total hipster places, with prayer flags hanging up and a real coffee machine behind the bar. I was sitting with a spicy chai, when I saw a flyer on a table: *Spoken Word nights, every Thursday at 7:00 pm. Come share your work!*

Before I even dreamed of writing a book, I was obsessed with writing poetry. I loved to write it. Loved to listen to it. It was therapeutic to me, a way to express my deepest inner self.

And it was Thursday. Perfect. I figured it might be worth it to come listen to some readings.

That night when I arrived, it was packed! There were hip people from every corner of the Earth. Some with friends. Some alone, like me.

I sat at a small, quiet table in the back corner. I was holding my poem; although I had no interest in reading it. These were strangers, and I never read my poems out loud. They're too personal. And not very good. But I had it with me anyway.

The night began, and slowly some people got up, one at a time, and read their work. Some read poetry about their lives, their views, their challenges. Some read spoken word about struggles in society. Some wrote nice stories about their travels. Some people played guitar, sang, rapped. I sat sipping my chai, feeling totally content. I felt inspired. Those people were like me, alone, traveling, a bit lost, ready to bravely share their stories and feelings with this closed group of strangers. Everyone was so supportive. So positive.

I felt safe.

A young man in dread locks and an old band t-shirt approached the mic. "Alright, guys! Thanks for sharing! So, who's next? Mic is free for someone else who wishes to share…anyone?"

The room was quiet.

I timidly raised my hand.

"Great! You! Come on up here!"

Everyone started clapping and cheering.

I slowly approached the mic. When I turned to look at the audience, I noticed there were more people watching than I initially thought.

What am I doing? This is so embarrassing. My poetry sucks.

I looked down at my poem and began to read. I never looked up from my notes once.

Everyone stayed silent.

Same routine, different day, trying to be happy, but life gets in the way.

What's the point in working for money you never spend, on anything other?

Than meaningless items and bills with no end?

Is that the point of life? Just living for tomorrow?

No raw, passionate joy, just a dull entrapment of sorrow?

My eyes finally opened the day I bought my first ticket,

I opened a new life, with love, adventure, and wonder in it.

Flying afar, to a mysterious place so unknown,

Some place wild and free, with a feeling of contentment in being alone.

How can you compare the sounds of traffic, to that of waves splashing up on a shore?

Driving to the office gives you money, but the sounds and beauty of nature gives

you so much more.

You can wrap your body in rich fabrics of silk and cashmere,

But do you think that will make joy and happiness suddenly appear?

I can assure you that climbing that mountain and standing higher than a cloud,

Will fill your heart with passion, and make your soul truly proud.

Your mind will not feel enlightened watching that show on your new flat screen.

Those repetitive images won't hurt you to go unseen.

Have you ever walked along the beach and watched the orange sun set on the shore?

The wonders of mother Earth are what makes your soul scream out for more.

Do all those clothes hanging in your closet, and all your shoes on the rack,

Ever take away the stresses, or all the burdens off your
back?
Owning very little, but experiencing every day,
Is what lights me up inside, what guides me along the
way.
Exploring a new village, wondering through a jungle of
rich green,
Going on new adventures, and dreaming of the sights
that still go unseen.
Not finding happiness in a pay-check, but just the simple
joys in a simple day,
The beauty in nature all around you, and the amazing
people you meet along the way.
The ever-changing days, greeting each one as brand
new,
Finding happiness in the simple things, and to yourself
you are true.
I say goodbye to the rat race, to the chase that has no
end,
And I welcome new adventures; for happiness is no
longer pretend.

When I was done, I looked up, and everyone started smiling, and cheering, and clapping. I smiled a huge smile.

Did they actually like it?

After that day, I felt incredibly inspired. Sharing my private stories and thoughts was such a vulnerable thing to do. It's you, your feelings, your fears, your dreams, your perceptions, raw, right there for everyone to hear. It's like opening up your heart, with no filters or barriers, for others to see and judge. But it helps. It encourages. There's nothing more amazing than finding out other people share your deepest darkest feelings. That you're not alone in the world. Feeling lost? Feeling alone? Feeling unsure? Feeling happy and not sure how to express it? That's okay. Me too.

I knew from then on, I would never keep my writing secret again. Whether it be for others, or just for myself, I would share it. I would put out there.

Thank you, Pai.

Chapter 8

China

In 2016, two major things happened in my life; I left Cambodia, and I moved to China. Guangzhou, to be specific. I got a job teaching English to adults at an English center; it would be good money, so a chance for me to save a bit, and travel more.

Leaving Cambodia was the hardest thing I had ever done. I loved my life there. I was surrounded by wonderful people, and my days were constantly filled with wonder, awe, and adventure.

Cambodia made me a better person.

Going to the airport broke my heart into a million pieces. I couldn't stop crying. My brain knew it was time to move on, but my heart ached to stay.

I believe a piece of my soul stayed behind forever.

But there's only so long you can live from day to day, without any plans or goals for the future. I knew I needed to move forward and build my career. And I knew I needed to see more of the world. I applied to many different schools all around Asia, from Japan to Korea, but China seemed to stick to me. I received an immediate response from the school in Guangzhou, and the process from that point forward seemed to run extremely smoothly.

Sometimes you need to listen to fate; somethings seem meant to be.

First arriving in China was totally different than arriving in Cambodia; Guangzhou was massive. It was a city as tall as it was wide. Sky scrapers towered over me, roads flooded with traffic, people were everywhere, off to work, off to the mall. Malls! Malls were everywhere. Massive ones, as big as every mall in Ottawa put together.

There were no back packers biking around like in Siem Reap. No dusty roads, no bamboo bars, no water buffalo wandering the streets or monkeys trying to steal your food. It was just urban grandiosity. It was as if I had stepped into the future. I felt overwhelmingly energized; it was the biggest city I had ever been to.

I planned on staying a year or two; save some money, and do the city life thing. I had no idea what to expect, or if I would be able to handle the responsibility and lifestyle. But I was open and excited for the new chapter.

I started training for my new job right away. It seemed more professional and stringent than the schools I was used to, but I caught on quite well, learned the new ropes, and made some good friends.

The thing I cherished about Guangzhou the most; my first big girl apartment. My boss set me up with an English-speaking realtor, and I found the nicest little one bedroom I could ever ask for. On the fifteenth floor, it had massive windows overlooking the city below, there was a modern bathroom (no squatty potties for this adult!), a flat screen TV, a cute kitchen, and queen-sized bed in the bedroom. Even luckier, there was home décor store right down the road...so damn, did I ever decorate it up!

It became my sanctuary. I spent most nights relaxing at home, having a glass of wine after work, watching a DVD, doing the dusting and washing. It was a homey place. Guangzhou was a slower paced, easier time for me. I could breathe there. I planned to work as much as I could, have a nice home to relax in, and then spend as much extra time and money travelling as I possibly could.

Those were my China focuses.

My heart and soul missed Siem Reap, and deep down I knew I wasn't a big city, nine-to-five working stiff; but for a couple of years, I needed it. And I embraced it.

While from the outside, my life seemed somewhat normal, everyday I was reminded that I was living in China, and something that would be super easy back in your home country, was a marathon somewhere else. One major issue was the language barrier. I learned a little bit of Mandarin during my years in Guangzhou, but not enough to really feel comfortable doing day to day errands. Taking a bus, getting the groceries, even just hailing a cab, were all things that became ten times harder in a country where your native language is obsolete.

One time I wanted to pick up some shampoo at the store, and I wanted a specific kind that is for dry hair. But when I went to the shampoo section, even though I found my brand, everything on the bottles were written in Chinese. I had no idea which one was for dry hair, oily hair, curly hair, or limp hair. When an employee walked up to me, I had to mime 'dry hair.' That was difficult. I kept making scratching sounds as I rubbed my hair, and she just looked at me like I was a crazy foreigner. Eventually she understood what I was trying to say and pointed to the right bottle. I smiled and said "Thank you" in Mandarin (one of the few phrases I actually knew) and tried to memorize the Chinese symbol for 'dry' for next time.

That basically was how every single shopping experience went for me.

In another more serious situation, I got a bit sick one day. I had a runny nose for weeks, and I just knew I had a sinus infection. Thank you, WebMD!

I went to the pharmacy and handed the pharmacist a note written in Mandarin that a co-worker wrote for me, that said 'Sinus infection—anti-biotics please.' He brought me back three separate packs of medicine, none of which I could read, of course. He tried to explain the differences to me, but I couldn't understand. I just pointed to my nose and then pointed to 'anti-biotics' on the note. He nodded and kept trying to speak to me, but it went nowhere. Using my online translator, I got a bit more information, and ended up buying two, just in case.

I started one pack, that I chose at random, and within 24 hours I felt worse! I woke up feeling drugged up, my head was spinning, and I could barely see straight. I was terrified at what the heck was in that pack! I was terrified of more foreign hospital experiences. I went off it immediately, but then my sinus infection came back. So, nervously, a couple days later, I decided to try the other pack.

I hoped I wouldn't end up feeling worse again.

Two days later, my infection was completely gone, and I felt great! So, it was a worthwhile gamble.

I don't recommend taking medicine at random like that, but sometimes you just don't have a choice.

Lesson 328: Bring medicine with you from home when you move to a new country.

**

"So, what about for my holiday in October? What do you think?" Molly asked me as she took another sip from her beer.

Molly was a good friend I met shortly after arriving in Guangzhou; a fellow English teacher who also lived in the same building as me. We were sitting in our favorite brewery down town; a common hangout for the expats in that city.

While I had been living in Asia for a few years already by that point, Molly was new to that side of the world. She had just moved to Asia earlier that year.

"Well, if you only have five days, I would suggest Penang or the Perhentian islands. Malaysia is amazing! It depends if you want more of an artsy scene, or just some beach time."

During my first couple of years in Asia, I met so many inspiring travelers. People who had visited numerous countries. People who had seen amazing places and done amazing things.

People who encouraged me to keep travelling. To keep seeing more.

I got so much advice from those people; friends and strangers alike. They gave me guidance on places to visit, gave me tips about beaches or towns far less travelled by other tourists.

Now there I was, passing on the torch.

Sharing tips and advice about places I had been. Inspiring someone else to see more.

Molly smiled at me. "God, Veronica, you really should write a book one day."

***

As the months rolled on, and my days became a bit more routine, I began to learn more and more about Chinese culture.

What I began to notice, and what amazed me, was how Guangzhou was so modern, so futuristic, so pristine and advanced; yet the people seemed to be twenty years behind. The city, and most of the country, had been growing so fast, advancing and progressing beyond most other countries, but the people struggled to keep up.

It was a city of modernity, but with people of traditionality. Tradition can be lovely sometimes, but other times it can be backward and suppressing.

I learned a lot about this through my students; they taught me just as much as I taught them. Women struggled. They had it tough. And because of the suppressing and controlling government, they didn't know how to be vocal about it and fight back.

At the school I worked at, seventy percent of the students were female. Country wide. It was an interesting statistic, and one I would often ask my students for discussion questions; why do you think seventy percent of the students here are women?

I grudgingly had to hear some of the men answer:

"Because women have more free time than men."

"Because men work harder at the office."

"Because men are smarter and speak better English."

But the truth, as I slowly learned, was because women had to work much harder in the workplace than men for the same outcome.

Equality just did not exist.

I learned from students that common interview questions for a woman candidate would be: Are you married? Do you have kids? Do you want kids?

It was perfectly legal.

The reason they asked this was because if a woman was single or married with no kids, they most likely wouldn't hire her because they were worried she would become pregnant soon and request maternity leave.

Now don't get me wrong, men had to work hard as well; pressures with money, success, and family was a struggle, of course, but Chinese women had much tougher expectations: Get married; get a good job; buy nice things; wear expensive clothes; have a son; take care of your children; cook delicious dinners; take care of your in-laws; be skinny; be pretty.

If they were unmarried, or childless, they were deemed left over women. Forgotten women. They felt and were told they were worthless.

One female student actually said to me once, "My father says I'm not married because I'm not pretty enough." It was heartbreaking to hear. And she said it so matter-of-factly.

I also noticed, after talking to so many female students, that most of them had children to please their in-laws. Having children, or a son preferably, was an obligation. A requirement. Not a joyful life decision you made with your partner. Life didn't seem to be about choice or freedom. It seemed to be about what was expected of you.

As an unmarried and childless woman myself, and one who embraced it, a lot of female students confided in me. They were China's strong, independent, feminist women, but had no public platforms on which to share their frustrations.

One married woman, I will call her Lee, sat in the classroom with me one evening.

"What do your mother and father say to you about not having a husband?" she asked me.

A question that made me put down my book.

"Um, well, nothing I guess. They are proud of me travelling and working. Getting married is not a priority."

"You are so lucky."

Lee was married and had an eight-year-old son. "I wish I never got married sometimes."

"Oh? Why do you wish that, Lee?"

"I wish to work. I used to be an editor and I was so good at it! But when I got married, my husband made me stop and says I only can take care of our son."

This is a very common situation in China. Women are expected to breed and cook. That's all. Men make the money.

"I am so sorry, Lee," I didn't even know how to respond to that. "But you should be proud. You are learning a new language, you are so smart, and you are doing some wonderful things. All on your own."

I tried to make her feel better, but I couldn't. Her situation broke my heart; her entire life in a loveless marriage to an awful, controlling husband.

I had another kind student named May. May was single, felt pressure from her family about it, but was strong and determined to find a good job and move to The United States. But one problem she faced; she didn't have a passport.

In my world, passports are easy. You go to a passport office, they make sure you're not some wanted criminal, then you get a passport. Easy. Done.

Not in China though.

Chinese people need government permission to own a passport. They have dozens of hoops to jump through to get one, everything is asked from previous jobs, hobbies, income, savings, reasons for travel...it's not a right to travel in China. It's a privilege bestowed on only the upper class.

May tried three separate times to get a passport but was always denied.

"What happened?" I asked. "Is there something you can try next time?"

"No. It is because I do not make enough money. They think I will not come back to China."

If they do get a passport, Chinese people can't even apply for visas on their own. The government has to do it for them. After they get approved to even apply.

If I want to go to another country, I just go. Even if I need a visa, I just go to the embassy, and get a visa, and go. Chinese people need their government to apply for them, so they have complete control over where they go, how long they stay, and when they come back.

No spontaneous European backpacking trips for them.

They can't even go to Hong Kong without government permission.

Another student who talked to me a lot about her situation was Eva.

Eva was a university student; young, sweet, dreamy-eyed, ambitious. She had dreams to travel, see the world, and kick ass doing it. She wanted to be a web designer and was working hard to make it happen.

The only problem she faced was her father. He, of course, was a traditional man. She wanted to go away for school, but wasn't allowed. She wanted to study art in school, but wasn't allowed. She wanted to take a design program in England one summer, but she wasn't allowed to even apply. Her father already had her whole life planned for her. And his word goes. She was an only child, and being under her parents roof forever, even after getting married and having kids, was mandatory.

I don't know what will happen to Eva. I hope her light never dims. I hope her dreams are still strong today. I hope she becomes a designer one day.

"Sometimes I wish I was born in Europe or something…I wish I could see how different my life could be," she said to me once.

"Well, Eva, we only have this one life, so don't let it go to waste."

She smiled at me, with her mouth, not her eyes.

Not everyone at the school was traditional though. Most students were young, liberal, open minded, and so curious to the world beyond the boundaries society had given them. Men and women alike.

We would have social events at the school sometimes, just a chance for the students to practice their conversational skills. Every time I would host an event, I made sure the topic was something they never got a chance to talk about outside. 'Gender roles,' 'unmarried couples,' 'travel,' 'dating,' 'cultures around the world...' they gobbled it down! They felt safe at the school. No judgement.

No boundaries. No rules. Just freedom.

We talked about anything they wanted. I made my open-minded views on life very clear, and they loved it.

The one struggle I had there as a teacher though; they were never taught how to think for themselves.

In school growing up, I was always taught how to think outside the box. *Which character do you connect with and why? How would you change the ending? What is one invention our world needs? Design your own village!* This is common in our schools.

In Chinese schools, 2+2=4. That's it. Problem and solution. Rote learning. Repeat, repeat, repeat. Get good grades. Go to university. It was almost robotic. They were never pushed to use their own unique abilities. They never got a chance to learn about themselves or their unique skills. They never got a chance to find their own passions.

Get good grades. Memorize everything. Find a good job. That's all they knew.

I would try to incorporate creativity and individualism in my classes; to give them a chance to get imaginative. They loved it! When I would have crafts, they couldn't get enough. I'm talking about girls, boys, men, women—there were businessmen still wearing their suits after work sitting there, pasting glitter on their masquerade masks—they all treasured those events.

Their personalities came out so strongly over the next two years. I enjoyed every minute of it.

***

None of their educational struggles had anything to do with their abilities or intelligence, but the society they came from.

In the politics of the People's Republic of China, the *Central People's Government* forms one of three branches of power, the others being the *Communist Party of China* and the *People's Liberation Army*. They say they are democratic, but it's all just smoke and mirrors. Elections in China are based on a hierarchical electoral system, where local Congresses are directly elected, and all higher levels of Congress, up to the National People's Congress, are indirectly elected by the People's Congress from the level below. So, citizens might feel like they have a little say in their politics, but in reality, it's all run by a few people right on top.

They also have very little freedom, not just with travel, but with their day to day lives as well. Freedom of speech? Hell no. You say something bad about their president or government, and you'll disappear. Social media? Controlled. Voting? Meh. Protests? You're arrested!

But the worst part, they don't know anything about their own country. It is all propaganda; China is amazing! China is the best country in the world! Other countries are dangerous!

The Tiananmen Square protests of 1989, commonly known in mainland China as the June Fourth Incident, were student-led demonstrations in Beijing. I remember learning about it in school.

In what became known in the West as the Tiananmen Square Massacre, troops with rifles and tanks fired at the protesters trying to block the military's advance into Tiananmen Square. The number of deaths has been estimated anywhere from a few hundred to over ten thousand.

No one under the age of thirty knows anything about it. The ones who were alive during this brave demonstration of national pride, cannot talk about it.

Even Mao Zedong, the murderous dictator of China in the 1960s and 1970s, is not talked about. Most Chinese people refer to him as 'Great Leader Mao,' but know none of his horrors. Forty-five million people were killed during the 'Great Leap Forward' from 1958–1962. It was an effort made by the Communist Party of China, under the leadership of Mao Zedong, to transform China into a society capable of competing with other industrialized Western countries; a chance to overtake all capitalist countries and become one of the richest and most powerful nations in the world. However, it was a huge failure, due to a lack of proper planning from the central government. There was so much focus on industrial and trade advancement that other industries, such as farming, were completely ignored; a great famine caused the death of millions of Chinese people.

For some reason, the leaders forgot that food was needed to keep so many millions alive.

The total death toll for his full reign is estimated at around eighty million, including genocides in Tibet,

Xinjiang, and Inner Mongolia; outdoing both Stalin and Hitler.

Now, I'm not trying to disrespect another country, I do understand that they want to control over a billion people and keep the peace. China also does know how to do it; by making their people happy. There were parks everywhere, clean streets, beautiful buildings and malls, tons of nice restaurants, so many amazing activities to do. Chinese cities were astonishing!

'Here you go guys, a gorgeous park for your kids! And this mall! It cost us millions of dollars to build! Here's a new movie theater, and a walking path along the river, an amusement park, and even a skating rink. Enjoy! Just don't ask any questions.'

The only problem I have is that eliminating one's history, even if it's horrific, stops people from banding together. To know you survived something, that you and your people endured pain, war, horror, and ill treatment, creates a feeling of unity and pride. We did this. We are strong. We can overcome anything.

There is zero of that in China. No one seemed concerned about anyone else.

I was told when I first arrived that if I saw an old or sick person fall over, not to help them up. This is because it's commonly a scam; elderly people will pretend to fall, and when you try to help them up, they yell and claim you pushed them, and sue you for hundreds of dollars.

No joke.

I kept thinking to myself, *am I really living somewhere where I can't help an old, sick man off the ground?*

The whole country had a sense of loneliness to it. Everyone was looking out for only themselves. Pushing, shoving, me-first mentalities, get out of my way; these were all the norm. This is all because of the previous communist regime; under Mao, people were starving. They were dying. If you didn't get that last bowl of rice, you'd go hungry. If you didn't make it on that train, you weren't going home. People fought for survival. It's understandable. And today, those people are seniors, and they have passed on those traits to their children, and their children after. Since no one truly knows the horrors of Mao and the Communist party, no one understands why! People shove, people push, people fight for something on the shelf at the store. That's just the way it is. There's no reason behind it to them, it's just the way of life.

It is common practice in China for the grandparents to raise the grandchildren. While moms and dads were off working all day, their parents oversaw the child's upbringing.

Growing up, I believe, most children are taught how to be polite and courteous in society. Excuse mes, pardons, sorrys; these are driven into our minds at an early age from our parents. However, children in China were taught the opposite.

I remember seeing older women dragging their grandchildren behind them, pushing and shoving to get onto the bus. I saw this on a daily basis. If getting on the last train or fighting for that last bowl of rice meant pushing people out of the way to feed their families, then so be it. That trait was then passed on to their children, and grandchildren.

There was no time for compassion. No time for politeness and etiquette. Survival of the fittest was their way of life. In effect, their 'rudeness' is a characteristic we might often misconstrue; It's not a lack of empathy, it is a struggle for survival for them.

I did notice a big difference in the younger generation though. They were polite. They said excuse me, and good afternoon. They smiled. Some men would get up and give me their seat. Some held the door open. Some moved out of the way for old women getting on the bus. They always helped me when I was lost. They always tried to speak English with me, and never made me feel like an intruder in their country; my presence always felt welcomed.

In modern day China, there is a lot of Western influence. They have an internationally focused mindset.

China is an international country now. Some Chinese people work for Western companies, they watch Hollywood movies, many travel abroad, even study with Western teachers. They think differently. China is in a constant change of flux; it is always adapting.

Those two years ended up being a huge opportunity for me to learn about human nature and see a bit of the beautiful country.

Chapter 9
China

Due to my love of the movie Avatar, one of my first trips was to Zhangjiajie; land of the famous sandstone columns, and the filming location of the movie's Hallelujah mountains.

Zhangjiajie is in Hunan Province, which is a poorer area in China; nothing like Guangzhou. There are no skyscrapers or million-dollar malls, only old villages, farmland, and dusty roads. It was night and day opposite.

After a long two-hour cab ride from the airport, I finally arrived at my homestay. As I got closer, the roads got dustier, the landscape wider, and the villages smaller. It was early in the morning; the sun was just rising over the flat, grassy horizon, turning the sky a misty yellow.

I stayed with a lovely family, right on their little farm. As I arrived, I was greeted by an old lady sitting on the front porch, smiling widely at me with her toothy grin, plucking feathers out of a dead chicken for supper.

"Hello!" smiled a pretty, young woman with a cute baby on her hip, standing behind the wooden desk. "Name?"

"Hello! My name is Veronica," I answered.

Her husband stood next to her, greeting me with a smile. I learned quickly that no one in the whole family, besides the wife, knew any English.

"Yes, okay; one room, four nights. Come with me."

She led me upstairs to my simple yet charming room, with a huge window overlooking the chicken coop and men farming in the dry fields below. This was not the China I was used to. How can one country have such richness in one city, and such poverty in another?

"When you ready, I cook you breakfast. Come down when ready," she then headed down the stairs.

I quickly washed up and headed down to the kitchen. There was a table set up next to the window, where two other guests were already sitting for breakfast.

"Morning!" we said to each other, as I sat to join them.

Breakfast was made up of rice soup, boiled eggs, Chinese bread buns, and tons of herbs and spices. I could see Grandma outside cooking the chicken she just plucked clean.

"Hello! I'm Veronica, nice to meet you."

"Hello! I'm Cam and this is Jon!"

"Where are you guys from?"

"Germany. And you?"

"Canada."

We ate our fresh breakfast and got to getting to know each other a bit. They were brother and sister, travelling around China for a few weeks in between job contracts. After a cup of Chinese tea, we decided to head out together to do some hiking in the famous Zhangjiajie National park.

After a bumpy bus ride to the starting point, we started our long trek up one of the mountains. Those mountains were special because they're not triangular, they're rectangular. Due to oceanic erosion millions of years ago, the mountains shoot straight up to the sky, with tall green trees perched right on top; it was like nothing I had ever seen before.

We hiked through forests and around the mountain, circling it upward bit by bit. A few sweaty, exhausting hours later, we finally reached the top. Cam, Jon, and I stood there next to the fence, looking out in astonishment at the views from so high up. The green mountain peaks covered the land as far as the eye could see, jolting up straight into the sky like blades of grass. It looked breathtakingly unreal; nature is truly amazing.

Jon pulled out his map.

"So, I think instead of walking right back down, we can keep walking that way and head down another mountain. To see something different."

"Yeah, that sounds good to me," I answered.

We began the long but beautiful hike, down some new paths and through some different forests, naively thinking a couple of hours later we would be back at the bus stop.

For a little bit of background information, Zhangjiajie National Park is eighteen and a half square miles of thick forests, confusing pathways, bus roads, and tall, scenic look-out areas. It is not a park that can be covered in one day, or even only on foot. Some areas are steep and inaccessible, or so spread out you need to take a shuttle bus from one area to another. To get around the park, you have to walk a while, sometimes up or down steep stairs, bus to another part, walk some more, then bus again, and so on.

It's quite complex. And easy to get lost or even go the wrong way.

This is also not explained in English anywhere in the park. Only Chinese.

After a few hours walking down the opposite mountain, we realized we got a bit lost. But that was okay, it's all part of the adventure.

We will find our way back soon, I thought. The sun was still out, birds were chirping. Other hikers were everywhere, and there were even the occasional monkeys swinging by. We stopped for a late lunch at a little vendor near a shuttle bus station and decided to hop on to explore some other areas.

Since we couldn't read any signs, and no one working at the park spoke English, we decided to go with our instincts; it makes sense that the buses would drive in one circular route, right? Eventually we would be dropped off back at the exit near our homestay. No worries.

We got off the bus at the first stop and got out to take some scenic photos and enjoy the sites. That area seemed much grander; with thicker mountains, and even a rushing river running through the trees. We stood there snapping away, while kids would sneakily come stand next to us, before running off.

Unlike Guangzhou, Hunan province was not international at all; westerners were a rare sight to see. Parents were telling their children to go stand next to us, the crazy looking alien-like foreigners with the light hair and weird faces, so they could quickly snap a picture.

This had happened to me a lot throughout my time in Asia, especially in small towns and villages. Foreigners were so mysterious to them, and even picture worthy in some cases. "Look everyone! Today I saw a real European person!"

It was all innocent; just pure curiosity and amazement, so I never minded it.

We did that for the next couple of hours, bus, walk, bus, walk, bus, walk. Aimlessly. Assuming we would eventually end up at our starting point again.

By the late afternoon, we were getting tired. The sun was hot. We were sweaty. We were ready to head back to the homestay.

"Guys, I think we should stay on the bus now and just wait until we get back to our exit," Cam suggested. We nodded in agreement. Sightseeing day was finished.

We sat on the bus, for what seemed like a long time, until we eventually got a bit anxious.

"I'm going to go ask the bus driver where we are," said Jon.

He walked up to the front of the bus, made an 'I'm confused' gesture with his hands, and pointed to the map. The bus driver pointed to it as well, then Jon walked back to us.

"He seems to say we are here," and he pointed to a spot on the other side of the park from where we were supposed to be.

"Guys, we should get off and ask someone how to get back," I suggested.

So, we got off the bus at the next stop. It was a busy area full of Chinese tourists waiting for the cable car to take them to the top of another mountain. We looked around for a park employee, and when we found one, who of course, spoke zero English, we kept miming "I'm lost. How do we get here?" and pointed to our exit on the map. The lady seemed to brush us off, almost annoyed at the English speaking.

We found another employee who quickly pointed to a bus and mumbled something in Chinese.

"Should we get on that bus?"

"Umm, I guess?"

Doubtfully, we got onto the bus and drove a few more stops. We felt like we were driving further and further away! Eventually it stopped at a big park entrance and the bus driver made everyone exit. End of the line. We got off in frustration and went to another park employee. He just quickly pointed to another bus, before walking away.

How the hell are we supposed to get back?

Tourists were all leaving the park, walking out in groups. Night fall was coming soon. The park closes early. We rushed into the ticket office, hoping someone could help us.

"Excuse me, do you speak English?"

"Little."

"We need to go here," Jon said as he pointed to the map.

"That is far. Only bus go."

"Okay! Which bus?"

"Bus over there," she dismissively pointed to the parking lot where we just walked out off.

We ran back and looked for a bus, any bus, that would take us back to our exit. But all the buses were parked and empty. The drivers had all left. Their shifts were over.

We quickly rushed back to the ticket office. They were clearly packing up to leave for the day.

"No buses! How can we get back?"

We were all feeling a bit panicky now.

"Bus only."

"But there are no more buses!" I exclaimed in frustration.

"Try taxi or public bus."

Outside of the park we saw tons of city buses parked. Nothing was written in English.

We wandered around the parked city buses, looking for anyone who might speak English. Not a soul. Only local people eager to get home. We walked up to some bus drivers and showed them our map, pointing to our far away homestay. They all hurriedly shook their heads and pointed further out into the city. Not one bus driver seemed to go to that area.

We were miles and miles away.

We walked into the little city, full of rushing cars and restaurants cooking out on the streets. The smells of meat and boiling vegetables filled the air. Dinner time.

I started to feel hungry.

"Guys, what about a taxi? Let's just split on one and get back to the homestay, I'm too tired to search for buses anymore," I said.

Cam agreed, "Yeah, I'm totally fine with that."

We hailed a taxi, and when we pointed to our homestay on the map, he seemed to laugh, then took out his phone and typed in a number.

500

"500 RMB, are you serious?" That's equivalent to about one hundred Canadian dollars, but none of us had even close to that on us. He drew a circle with his finger on the map, showing us the route, he would have to take to get there. All around the national park. A long trip.

All of a sudden, a young teenage girl overheard us and walked over.

"Excuse me, can I help you?"

Bless the children.

"Yes! Oh my god, we need to get here," Jon pointed on the map. "Can you help?"

"Um I think a bus can get you here," she pointed half way, to another park exit. "That exit maybe has buses I think. Those buses maybe take you to your hotel."

At that point, anywhere was closer than where we were.

"I show you."

The young girl walked us a couple of blocks to a dirty, crowded bus station, with lines of exhausted people waiting to get onto buses.

"That one will take you," she pointed and smiled.

"Thank you so much!"

We lined up, then double checked by pointing to the exit on our map to the driver. She nodded.

"Yes! Okay guys, at least we'll be closer to our homestay than we are right now," said Jon.

"One step at a time is fine with me!" I happily responded.

We walked on to the little bus, full of people holding babies, groceries, and back packs. They looked at us in complete confusion.

The bus drove for about thirty minutes, before the driver motioned at us to get out.

Please let us have gone in the right direction, I thought.

We got out at another park exit. It was much smaller than the other one, but busier. This exit had dozens of people walking out into the parking lot. We were the only ones walking in. I quickly scanned the crowds for possible English speakers. None.

The sky was rapidly getting darker. I was feeling hungry. We were all feeling incredibly frustrated.

We walked into the park and found the ticket office.

"Can you speak English?"

The woman at the desk looked at us, hiding a snicker.

"Can you help us?"

Blank stare.

"We need to go here!" Jon threw down the map in annoyance and pointed to our exit.

She shook her head. Said nothing.

I made a phone with my hands, "Phone please?" I took out our homestay's business card from my wallet. "Maybe we can call the owners and they can explain to us how to get back? The wife speaks a little English."

Jon and Cam looked momentarily hopeful.

The ticket office lady came back and handed me her phone, and I quickly dialed the number.

"*Nihao!*" I yelled when she picked up. "It is Veronica. We are lost. Help us?"

"Where?"

I handed the lady the phone, and they spoke for a couple of minutes, before she handed it back to me.

"Yes, walk, take bus, walk, stairs, bus, home."

"Um, okay, where is the bus?"

"Bus. Yes."

"What bus?"

110

"Park bus."

It was getting nowhere. We hung up.

"Where is the bus?" I made a bus gesture with my arms, but the lady just stared blankly at us.

"Damn it, guys, what are we going to do?" Cam shouted.

No one spoke English. No one even seemed to care to help us. It was dark now. The park was closing. No buses seemed to be running.

We didn't know if we should risk trying to walk back, miles away, in the pitch-black forest. It didn't seem like a good idea.

"How much money does everyone have?" Jon asked.

We all counted our cash. 200 RMB total. Not enough for a taxi. Or even a hotel.

Wow we might have to sleep in the woods.

We walked back outside and saw a small police station and hurried over.

Of course, they didn't speak any English. The cops began talking to each other, probably trying to figure out what to do with us.

We all sat on the curb. Lost. Scared. Defeated.

We were running out of options.

But then, I heard a miracle speak to us.

"Hello? Do you need help?"

I looked up and saw a young Chinese man looking at us concerningly. I may have jumped on him.

"Yes! We are lost! We need to get to our hotel! Can you help us?"

"Yes, but I don't know the directions."

"Can you speak to the people at our homestay?"

"Yes, no problem."

He asked the police men for a phone, and I dialed the number. He spoke Chinese with them, looking around, describing our location.

"Okay, he says to stay here. He will come get you. Stay here though. He said maybe thirty minutes."

"Thank you, thank you, thank you!" we all shouted as he smiled and walked away.

One thing traveling has taught me; sometimes you need to believe in the kindness of strangers.

We sat there, in the dark, with a couple of police officers, just vulnerably hoping that we would be rescued.

We eventually saw a flashlight approach us from through the trees. There he was, the nice husband from our homestay. Our knight in shining armor!

"*Nihao!*" he said. We ran to him, like lost puppies. "Thank you!"

We followed him through the forest, walking for about ten minutes, before we got to a lone bus sitting in an empty nighttime parking lot. The bus took us somewhere, who knew in that pitch darkness, and we got out and walked up some steep, stone stairs. It was pitch black out at that point, and I could barely see a couple feet in front of me. At the top we took another bus down a mountain, to the exit, and walked back to our homestay.

There would have been no way we could have figured that out alone!

The moment we walked into our homestay, with the grandma and wife preparing food and boiling tea, I couldn't have been happier.

We crashed into the chairs at the kitchen table and ordered a feast.

"You okay?" the wife asked us.

"Yes, thank you for saving us!"

They both smiled and handed us some cold beer.

We all sat there, sipping our beer, resting our feet, and thanking the heavens that Zhangjiajie didn't swallow us up whole.

***

Of course, like any good traveler, I did the major Chinese sites throughout my time there; The Great Wall in Beijing, the Pandas in Chengdu, the old teahouses in Shanghai, and the classy bars in Hong Kong. But I have always preferred nature to cities, so I made sure I took time to head far west; to China's Yunnan Province.

I first arrived in Kunming and knew right away I would have a hard time leaving. The city was quaint and quiet, with old houses and buildings, all surrounding a pristine lake. There were bright green parks, cozy tea houses, lotus ponds. People were charming, friendly, and slow-paced. I enjoyed my time exploring and wandering those streets.

Until I decided to take a train to the famous rock forest.

Travelling the world is amazing, but travelling the world alone as a single female is a bit of another story. As much as I hate to say it, it's a man's world. Being a woman off on the road can be scary at times; it's riskier, scarier, and messier. We always have to have our guard up. We must keep one eye open. We need to watch who we trust.

Even though this is the horrible reality we must face, I am a strong believer in doing what's in your heart; never let the world tell you what you can and cannot do. I will never let society scare me from doing something I dream of.

"It would be safer with a man." "You should travel with a boyfriend more." "It's not safe for girls like you." "You shouldn't go there." "You can't protect yourself there." "Who will take care of you?"

I will. I will take care of me.

My goodness, I hated those questions.

Why is it so difficult to understand that some people actually enjoy doing things on their own? And that the best adventures and most amazing memories come out of situations that scared you?

But like every girl on this planet, I have encountered the odd chauvinistic, sexist, women-alone-deserve-harassment thinking assholes here and there. That day at the Kunming train station I encountered two of them.

I was sitting in a huge, almost empty outdoor waiting area, just quietly reading my book. Two young guys came over and sat on either side of me.

I ignored them and continued to read.

"Where you going?" one asked.

I just kept on reading.

They moved closer.

"Where you going? You alone?"

I looked up at them, gave them a *screw off* face, then continued reading.

They moved closer.

"Why you alone? You have boyfriend?"

"Please get away from me."

"Why, we just want to talk to you."

I got up to move, and they got up with me. I quickly sat down.

I wasn't feeling annoyed anymore, I was a bit intimidated. *Should I try to run? What if they grab me? Is anyone else even around right now?*

"Leave me alone." I tried to look angry.

"You need boyfriend."

"No, I don't. Go away."

"Where you going?"

They were getting persistent. And more hostile.

"Hey Liana, we're going to grab a cup of coffee before our train, you comin'?"

I looked up and saw a young woman standing in front of us. She had a dark pony tail, an Australian accent, and a look of concern in her eyes.

At first, I had no idea who she thought I was, but then I realized what she was doing. She was coming over to a stranger in a tough situation, pretending we were friends, and getting me away safely.

She understood.

She had probably been there before.

The guys just stared at her. Then at me. They felt powerful against one woman. But two? Or more? Nope.

"Um, yes, sounds good. Coming!"

I stood up and we walked away together.

I later learned her name was Morgan. Morgan, if you ever read this, thank you for helping me out that day. You didn't have to, but you chose to get a fellow female traveler out of an uncomfortable situation.

Sisterhood is so important.

***

A few days later, I arrived in Dali; the cutest, most charming mountain city I had ever seen. Dali is known for its beautiful lake, full of mangroves and rocky beaches, and its surrounding red-clay mountains.

I spent a few days just walking the cute streets, browsing little handmade shops, and sipping tea in tiny, quaint cafes. It was so quiet, and so calm for China. I absolutely loved it.

One afternoon, I was in my favorite café in Dali, writing in my journal and drinking Chinese red tea. Sitting next to the window, I could smell the post-rain on the stone sidewalks, and hear someone playing a Chinese *Leiqin* in the street.

The owner of the café came over to me and refilled my tea pot. He was so nice and spoke quite decent English; uncommon in that area of China.

"What are you writing, miss?"

"Just writing my stories in my journal."

"Very nice. You like to write in your journal?"

"Oh yes, very much! I have been writing in journals since I was eighteen. I have many journals back home."

He smiled at me. "Wow that is good. So where is home?"

"Canada."

His eyes widened.

"Canada? Wow amazing. My sister lives in Canada."

"Really?" I asked.

"Yes, she is a doctor in Canada. Oba. Otta...Otat..."

"OTTAWA?"

"Yes, Ottawa! Capital! She went to Canada to study thirty years ago. Now she is a doctor at Ottawa General Hospital for twenty years."

There I was, sitting in a café across the world. In a city most people haven't ever heard of. As far from home as I could ever be. And I was talking to a Chinese man whose sister lives in my hometown.

What an amazingly small world.

**

Living and travelling in China, I learned so much about human nature; we all seem so different, yet we are all the same.

We all want happiness. We dream of better jobs, nicer homes, and a better life for our kids. We have fears. We have desires. We have likes and dislikes. We all believe in something.

But we are just the consequences of our society. We are the victims of our own fates. We adapt and learn based on the boundaries life gives us, but all still dream of more. Some of us might be born into lives of luxury, freedom, and privilege, while others fight tougher battles and get less opportunity. This might help us pave the road we then take in life; however, our humanity, passion, and nature are all still there. Still the same.

Nature and nurture, I believe, working hand in hand.

Chapter 10

Nepal

After over five years of calling Asia my home, knowing it was coming to a bittersweet end, I thought it would be best to finish it with a bang. I quit my job a month early, and flew to Nepal, before the final flight home.

I was craving adventure, especially after two years of living in a huge metropolis. A few months prior, I heard about the Annapurna trek in Nepal; a two-week long hike through the Himalayas, and over the Annapurna pass. Also known as the tallest pass in the world. It stuck with me. I knew I had to do it.

An adventure of a lifetime.

I took weeks beforehand preparing; unlike my hike on Rinjani. I bought good gear, proper clothing, lots of layers, snacks, a medical kit, appropriate trekking boots, waterproof cover ups; I was ready!

I read mixed reviews about getting a guide, especially if you're hiking it alone. In the end, I decided to opt out of hiring one. Most likely, I would meet other trekkers on the trails anyway. Plus, I wanted to do it alone; I felt I needed time to test myself, really get back to nature, and push my limits. Sometimes one needs adventure, and even a bit of danger, to truly feel alive.

This was my last trip in Asia! I wanted to make it count.

I was a bit nervous; I will admit. On the plane I kept thinking, *people die in situations like this you idiot! What if you don't meet anyone else? What if something happens? What if you get hurt?*

But I never back out of anything because of fear; fear has always seemed to drive me. Imagine how boring life would be if you didn't do things you that scared you?

Why is that? Maybe because I think we shouldn't fear fear, we should embrace it. Fear challenges us. Fear gives us memories worth making.

Without fear, you would never have bravery. Without bravery, you could never have adventures.

The best things that have ever happened in my life began with fear; moving to Cambodia, moving to China, climbing Rinjani, travelling alone to secluded places. Fear has always motivated me. I knew I would come out of those mountains a changed person.

And I did.

I first arrived in Kathmandu, where I would stay for a couple of days before heading to the mountains. The energy of the city hit me full force.

It was absolute chaos.

Rickshaws raced around the streets, prayer flags hung everywhere overhead, small buildings jammed together, people rushing about, shops full of souvenirs, the smells of curry and spices filled the air.

I was in love again.

It reminded me of my first love, Siem Reap; but even more vigorous. More bustling. More energetic.

I checked into my tiny hostel in the back-packer district, and immediately hit the streets. The liveliness in the air filled my veins with energy.

I began my sightseeing in the famous Durbar Square; home of Hindu temples and ancient stupas. There were people everywhere! Locals were lighting candles and incense outside of temples dedicated to Hindu Gods. People were selling food in little carts. And the pigeons! I had never seen so many pigeons! The whole cobble stone square was covered with them.

An absolutely perfect photo-op, I wandered over to the square, and I saw a few people throwing the pigeons food.

"We feed the pigeons because one day we will be born as pigeons, and we hope they will feed us," one man said to me as he threw corn kernels on the ground.

From a country that strongly believes in reincarnation, I found this beautifully moving.

I walked to the other side of the square to the temple of Kali. In Hinduism, Kali is known as the Goddess of destruction. Every year, locals in Kathmandu sacrifice hundreds of animals to keep her spirit at bay. Something that was particularity fascinating to me, was that they believed she reincarnates into the body of a young girl every few years.

The way they choose her is interesting. And a bit terrifying. A few baby girls are chosen, based on family name and history, and are put into a dark room for a whole day. The room has almost no light, and is full of animal blood and snakes slithering around. They watch the poor babies through a small window. The baby girls who are crying and acting frightened or hysterical are deemed mortal, but the one baby who is calmly sitting there playing in the blood must be Kali; for Kali would never be frightened of such things.

At the time I was in Kathmandu, Kali's reincarnation was about seven years old, named Kumari, and she lived with a priest family in a little house in Durbar Square. Her house surrounded a small court, and had tiny windows along the old, sculpted walls.

She would live there until she hit puberty. At that point, she would go back to live with her birth family, and another baby would then be chosen.

Photography was forbidden there.

I was in the small court, looking up at her windows, when she suddenly stuck her head out! I was entranced. She glared down, with her youthful face covered in red and black paint, and her eyes full of wisdom beyond her years.

I'm not a big believer in religion, or any gods, but at that moment, I kept thinking, *please don't hurt me Kali. Please allow me to have a safe journey.*

She then went back into her home.

I think she listened.

***

Two days later, I was on an old, rackety bus, heading to Besisahar; the starting point of the trek. Typical for Nepal, the bus ride that was supposed to be five or six hours long lasted more than ten. After a few hours sitting there relaxing with my music, enjoying the scenery out my window, the bus came to a sudden halt. There was a line of traffic in front of us, unmoving. Lines began to form behind us as well.

Ten minutes passed.

Then twenty. Then thirty.

We weren't moving.

Getting hot and sweaty just sitting there, and a bit impatient, I left the bus to walk a bit and see what was going on.

No one else had any idea.

I walked up the road, for about ten minutes, and I still didn't get to the cause of that traffic jam. There was nothing around us; just jungle, farm houses, and fields. Locals stared at me. I finally met a few other tourists, and we sat together at the side of the road for a while, chatting and passing time.

One hour passed.

Then two.

Still not moving.

It's hard to go with the flow sometimes, especially when you're used to your home country where everything runs on time, and questions are always answered.

Not in Nepal. Or most of Asia for that matter.

"What's happening?"

"A landslide I think."

"How much longer until we can drive again?"

"No idea."

I sat there with nothing to do, trying to stay positive, and soak up another travelling experience.

Don't get frustrated, I told myself, *It's all part of the adventure.*

***

After what felt like an entire day of waiting and busing, I finally arrived in Besisahar. My butt was asleep, my neck was sore, and man oh man was I ready to go! It was too late in the day to start hiking, so I got a hotel for the night.

In Besisahar is where I met Rikki. She was my age, traveling alone, and also planning on doing the Annapurna trek. And just like that I had my hiking buddy!

We bonded immediately. She was the coolest girl I had ever met—so adventurous and independent, interested in holistic healing and spirituality—her energy was inspiring, and I was looking forward to trekking with her.

The next morning at sunrise, we packed up our backpacks, tied up our hiking boots, and hit the road! We both felt so positive and ready for the trek.

We got this.

Rikki and I spent the first few hours getting to know each other; sharing the stories of our journeys. There's always something so encouraging when meeting another solo female traveler. Knowing you're not alone, and knowing that other people understand your views, motivations, and struggles, really makes you feel like you can keep going. You're on the right track. There are other people like you out there, don't worry.

"I've been working for a year back in Australia, saving every penny I could. I've been planning this trip forever, and now I'm travelling around Nepal for six whole months!" Rikki told me.

She had the travel bug too.

"We should stop in Bhulbule for a big breakfast, then we could probably make it to Bahundanda by the afternoon," I suggested.

"Yeah, good plan," Rikki replied. "We can stay there for the night and then trek to Chyamje tomorrow."

We gave ourselves a strict schedule to follow, to keep ourselves from straying too far, and not making the pass in time. It was low season, rainy season, and the weather was not on our side. It was hot. And humid. And by the afternoon the strong rains always hit.

We trekked through valleys and across bridges. There were tons of farmers working in their fields. Fields of every shade of green in existence.

That was the wonderful side to rainy season; everything was blooming.

We arrived in Bhulbule by mid-morning and found a little teahouse for breakfast. The sun was fully out by then, and would get stiflingly hot by noon.

"Hey girls! Doing the Annapurna hike as well?"

Rikki and I looked up from our bowls of banana porridge. There was a young guy standing there in his hiking gear, clearly alone and looking for hiking companions.

"Hey! Yeah, we are! You alone?"

"Yes, I am, I'd love to tag along if that's okay?"

"Sure!" Rikki smiled back.

He sat down with us, leaning his poles on the table and ordering some masala tea.

"My name is Jay, I'm from Pakistan. And you girls?"

"I'm Veronica, from Canada, and this is Rikki, from Australia."

Jay was young, around twenty-four years old. He was incredibly profound, spiritual, and so intelligent. He worked in women's clinics back in Pakistan, and hoped to get his

Master's degree in Holland the following year. He ended up being one of the most interesting guys I'd ever met. And later on, a really good friend.

Travelling gives you friends all around the world.

And the world doesn't seem so big and scary after that.

After breakfast, we continued our hike to Bahundanda, where we would spend the night. It was incredibly hot. The walk was continuously uphill. My back-pack was so heavy and my new hiking boots were giving me blisters. I had no idea how I would be able to do that for two straight weeks. But we stopped for breaks, chatted along the way, and kept ourselves motivated. The views were also quite breath-taking; the scenery was far and wide green mountains and valleys. There were picturesque farms everywhere, made of perfectly stacked stones and wooden logs. The thick, twisty trees around us were hundreds of years old. There were fields of horses everywhere. The air was clean and the sky was blue. Scenic nature at its best.

About five hours later, we finally arrived. The little village was on top of a tall hill, overlooking the fields below. There was only a handful of small homes along that one dusty road. No electricity.

We chose a small teahouse owned by a sweet Nepalese woman, named Laya. Laya wore a long yellow sari and had long dark hair down to her waist. Her tanned, wrinkled skin showed years of hard work and long days outside, but her bright eyes shone with beauty, youth, and wisdom.

It was low season, so we had the entire teahouse to ourselves! Most of the hike ended up being that way.

As soon as we arrived, bags were thrown on the floor, boots were kicked off, and *dal bhat* was immediately ordered. I sat there with Rikki and Jay, on that picnic table in the dark, wooden kitchen, rubbing our feet and necks with tiger balm, and wrapping our blisters with band aids.

We ate a huge lunch, then went upstairs to claim our beds. I spent the rest of the day laying on my bed next to the window, looking out at the majestic mountains we would be climbing, writing in my journal, and reading my book; it is definitely the little things in life.

By 8:00 pm we were all fast asleep. One day down, at least ten more to go.

***

We woke up at the crack of dawn the next morning, had a quick cup of masala tea with Laya, and the three of us hit the road again. Day two was a twenty-kilometer trek to Chyamje, about 1430 meters above sea level.

It was humid and blisteringly sunny. We hiked up trails through thick bush and river beds. We passed charming farms, full of colorful gardens and roaming chickens, and trekked through valleys in between rolling mountains. It was exhausting, yet stunning. I couldn't remember the last time I was surrounded by so much untouched nature.

We arrived in a small village called Ghermu for breakfast. The village was one long gravel road alongside the river, full of stone houses and farmers walking herds of mules up and down the road. After a hot bowl of porridge and boiled eggs, we continued another ten kilometers up along the mountain trails to our second overnight stop; a small mountain village called Chyamje.

"Hello! Welcome to Chyamje! Please stay at our home! We cook you nice dinner! We have comfortable beds for sleeping!"

As soon as we entered the village, a young man came rushing out of his house and greeted us. Low season brought very few hikers, and business was struggling.

It was the late afternoon and the rain was beginning to fall harder and harder. Our backs were sore, our feet throbbing; it didn't take too long to convince us.

Rikki, Jay, and I walked into his home and checked out the guestrooms—tiny beds with fresh sheets, pillows, and windows looking out onto the valley below—perfection.

"You guys alright with this place?" asked Rikki.

"I'm hungry, and I need a shower. This place looks like the Hilton as far as I'm concerned!" I happily answered as I already began untying my boots.

I washed up in their ice-cold outdoor shower, forgetting that hot water was a luxury in these parts, then Rikki and I hand-washed our clothes in a basin outside before hanging them to dry next to our window. It that humidity, we'd be lucky if they would get half dry by morning.

By the time we were all washed up, our dinner was ready. *Dal bhat* of course; a traditional Nepalese dish, made with lentil sauce, potatoes, pumpkin vine, and rice; healthy and filling.

We sat outside on the balcony, surrounded by trees, prayer flags, and the sounds of the rushing river.

"How are you guys feeling today?" Jay asked, scooping in another mouthful of *dal bhat*.

"Good actually," Rikki replied. "My hips are feeling sore from my back-pack, but I think I'll be fine for tomorrow."

"My feet are hurting a bit because of my blisters but feeling fine now after a shower and some good food!" I laughed as I took a sip of masala tea.

We spent the evening enjoying our absolute seclusion; no Wi-Fi, no TV, no other people. I wrote a lot, chatted with the teahouse owners, and we all fell asleep by nightfall.

I was away from everything. And it felt amazing. I had no idea what was going on in the world, whether it be a new political scandal or celebrity engagement. I had no contact with anyone, besides Rikki and Jay, nor could anyone contact me.

It was therapeutic.

Humanity in the Western world relies on technology to live. We need it. I don't remember ever seeing anyone back home without their smartphone on them twenty-four seven. It's how we work, how we stay in touch, how we show the world what we're doing and how successful we are.

We cannot avoid it, it's not even our fault. It's the direction the modern world is moving.

But when you're forced into a situation where technology is obsolete, you remember how to just live again. You live in your own head, in your own mind. You notice everything around you; you take things slower. Instead of whipping out your phone to snap a picture, you just stare at something long enough until it's in your long-term memory.

It was just me. And the real world. I was totally free.

***

We all woke up at dawn again, and left the comfort of our cute, safe little teahouse, and continued our trek. It was still dark and quite misty with rain.

"Guys, we have to cross over here I think," said Rikki, looking down at our map.

"Cross where? There's a huge river," I said.

We were in the middle of a bushy valley, next to the river, which flowed stronger and stronger the further we trekked.

The sun was slowly coming up.

"I think there's a bridge up here," Jay walked further on, and we came to a tiny, rackety bridge which crossed the river.

What am I? Indiana Jones?

"Is there another way across?" I asked.

Rikki laughed. "Only if you want to try swimming and fighting the river's currents!"

"Ok…I guess I'll go first?"

I held my poles tightly in one hand and gripped the rope hand rail with the other. The bridge swayed in the wind and was woven together with wooden planks and straw ropes.

Something out of an adventure film.

I crossed slowly, watching each foot, one at a time, step on one plank. Then another.

The river far down below rushed with strength and vengeance.

One plank. Then another.

When I touched land on the other side, I finally exhaled.

"Okay! Made it! Who's next?" I shouted across.

We made it to our third nights' stop in Dharapani. Another tiny village along one dusty riverside road. There were a few teahouses, all painted bright pinks and oranges, and a couple of little wooden shops.

"Guys, is that a chocolate bar?" I shouted as I ran toward a shop.

"Oh my gosh and they even have caramel ones!" Rikki smiled.

We bought some candy bars and checked into a little teahouse for the night.

A big *dal bhat* dinner, a few cups of masala tea, and two very delicious chocolate bars later, we were all fast asleep.

***

At dawn again the next day, we hit the road. It was rainy and a bit cool, and the ground was wet and muddy.

I felt tired, but it was like my body was slowly adjusting to the early mornings and extensive hiking.

That day was a long one; we ascended another seven hundred meters up and around mountains. The landscape was beginning to look different; there were pine trees scattered around the valleys, and the misty white clouds were floating over our heads.

I couldn't believe how high we must have already climbed.

"Guys…is that…marijuana?"

I looked up at Jay's question, and right ahead of us, no lie, were acres and acres of marijuana plants. Bright green, thick and bushy, towering over our heads.

"Is this a mirage?" I joked.

Rikki pulled out her map and then said, "Yeah, guys, these are the famous marijuana fields. They grow for miles and miles!"

We laughed and began trekking through the bushy fields, moving the plants out of our way. I couldn't see anything but marijuana leaves.

It was a stoners paradise.

"Can we just…"

"No, Veronica, they're not ready for picking yet," answered Rikki, knowing what I was going to ask.

"Ok…just wondering."

After a long, blind hike through the fields, we finally got to normal land again. For a while there I didn't think we'd ever find our way out. We began walking up the muddy trails, ready to tackle our next mountain, when Rikki stopped dead in her tracks.

"Oh no, guys," she bent over and picked at her shoe, "that's a leech."

I froze.

"What?"

"There are leeches on my shoes. Probably from those thick marijuana bushes."

"But we're not in water!" shouted Jay.

"Doesn't matter, it's wet and misty, they'll be latched onto the damp plant leaves. Everyone check your shoes and socks!"

I squatted down, and saw two baby leeches crawling up my shoe, and immediately flicked them off. I had never seen leeches before, and to be honest they were creatures out of my nightmares.

"Veronica, look in your socks too," she said to me, as both her and Jay began taking off their boots.

I peeled back my sock and saw him. A huge, juicy monster stuck to my ankle.

I yelled as I ripped him off my skin and wildly threw off my boots. "Ahh! They're everywhere!"

Rikki came up behind me and slapped me on the shoulder. "Welcome to the wilderness," she laughed.

Leeches stuck to my feet is something I doubt I will ever get comfortable with.

We continued to pull ourselves up through thick terrain, steep muddy trails alongside tree covered mountain slopes for another six hours, passing the odd cow pasture and busy farmer, before we finally made it to Chame! The air was wet, but quite cool.

We were getting higher, and the climate was getting colder.

The altitude was slowly beginning to hit me; my breathing felt shallower and my body a bit weaker.

I was feeling frailer than I did the day before.

And more exhausted.

My breathing was getting more and more difficult.

My feet were so sore, and I could feel my blisters start to bleed.

I was starting to worry if I was in over my head. If I would be able to finish the hike.

I'm a fivefootthree, hundred-pound girl, what am I doing out here? I kept thinking. *I have no real hiking or wilderness training.*

I was starting to worry, and starting to doubt myself.

Chame was a slightly bigger village than the others; there were a few more teahouses, many more little shops, and for the first time on our hike, we actually saw some other trekkers!

We checked into a cozy teahouse, threw off our bags, and fell into our beds.

I don't know if I was just extremely tired and sore, but it was the most comfortable bed I had ever laid in before.

The best part of that teahouse was that they had actual hot water! There was a small gas tank which heated the shower; something necessary in that cold altitude.

I stood under that hot water, letting it wash over my face, hair, and skin. Soothing my muscles.

What luxury.

Downstairs in the kitchen, the nice woman who owned the teahouse cooked us some hot *dal bhat*, then Rikki and I sat by the small fireplace all evening. We dried out our shoes, hung up our socks, and sipped tea as we felt our bodies slowly warm up.

"So, what's going on with you and that guy you were dating in Cambodia?"

"Cory?"

"Yeah, him."

I looked back into the fireplace, watching flames snap and crack at the logs.

"Well, it is what it is, you know?"

She stared at me to continue.

"We care about each other very much. I think we always will. We've been through a lot together."

"But…?"

"But I guess it's tough sometimes. You know, with both of our lifestyles. I'm in Asia, he's back home in England. I don't know where I'm going next, nor does he. It's tough to keep a long-distance relationship going when there's no end point in sight."

Rikki nodded as she took another sip of her tea. "Are you guys still together?"

"In a way, yes. But we need to be, I don't know, free? I need to have the ability to figure out where I want to go next. And he needs to figure out what he wants to do too."

Cory moved back to London when I left Cambodia. Neither one of us could imagine living in Siem Reap without the other. He got a good job there, and was spending much needed time with family, and I was on another path, working and traveling in Asia. I visited him in London few times, and he came to Guangzhou to see me a few times as well.

We were together. But also not together.

Relationships can have gray areas sometimes.

"I guess we want to be in each other's lives, but also need space to figure things out for ourselves."

Rikki smiled at me. "I totally understand. Good for you for doing what's best."

Like I said, wild people are impossible to be with, but also impossible to be without.

***

Later that evening, I was complaining to Rikki about my blisters and sore toes. We were sharing a room together, as we had been doing our whole hike.

"Let me see your feet," she said.

I took off my newly warmed up socks and showed her my feet. I had two massive blisters on both of my pinky toes. I also had one that opened and there was dry blood on my heel.

"Okay, those need to be popped and cleaned and wrapped!"

She put both my feet in her lap, got out her medical kit, and began cleaning up my toes. She popped my blisters, cleaned them with antiseptic lotion, and wrapped them up nicely.

"Thanks, Rikki!"

They felt better right away.

It's amazing how fast you bond with people whom you share intense experiences with. Rikki and I had only known each other for four days at that point, but had slept next to each other every night, changed in front of each other, told each other our deepest secrets and most personal stories, and even peed sitting next to each other.

Now there she was, cleaning up my gross, blistered feet for me.

I felt like I had known her for years.

It hadn't even been a week.

Adventure in the real wilderness and tough, physical struggles are truly bonding experiences. I need you. You need me. To get through this unscathed, we need each other. It's you and me, versus the mountains.

She had my back, and I had hers.

The friends you make in the Himalayas are friends you make for life.

Chapter 11
Nepal

I felt so energized the next morning. My feet were all bandaged up, my clothes warm and dry, and I even had a hot shower the night before; I was ready to tackle the next day of hiking!

The fifth day was not too strenuous, but probably the biggest change I had seen terrain wise. We seemed to have left behind all the bushy jungles and green fields, and entered the land of flat meadows, rolling valleys, and dry pine tree forests. There were apple orchards and sheep pastures, and we even came across the most amazing rock garden during our hike. In the middle of a huge pine forest, we hiked long paths covered with stacked rock stupas.

That is a common sight in Nepal; stacking stones—it's a meditative practice, to exercise one's patience and concentration—and the forest was covered with them! From other people, locals and trekkers alike, who stopped to stack their own little rock stupa.

Of course, Rikki, Jay, and I stopped to make our own.

It felt very calming and spiritual somehow.

We were all hiking along the trail, up on the side of a forest-covered mountain, when we came across a waterfall. It was cascading down a cliffside, and was loud and massive. It appeared to have broken away the bridge and flooded the trail.

The whole trail was covered in freezing glacier water, about a foot deep.

We stopped dead in our tracks.

I looked back. No bridge or side path.

We were hiking along a cliffside—no way to walk around the waterfall. The only way to continue down the trail was to walk through the fast-rushing water.

"Okay, everyone, shoes off I guess." shouted Rikki.

We began untying our boots and pulling off our socks.

As soon as I stepped into the water, it felt like a million tiny knives stabbed my skin. The water came from a glacier, and freezing cold doesn't begin to express how it felt. It was painfully numbing.

As I hurriedly walked through the water, carrying my boots, I yelled out in pain the whole way. I heard Jay and Rikki closely behind me shouting as well.

"You guys, this is brutal!"

"Oh, my god, my feet feel like they're on fire!"

As I walked, the flowing icy water splashed up on my legs. More knives and more stabbing pain.

I finally stepped out of the water, onto the dry trail again. My feet were burning with frigid cold stabbing pains.

How could cold water burn so much?

But when we all made it to the trail, we laughed. I tried to dry my numb, wet legs with a dirty shirt.

All part of the trek.

I quickly put my thick socks back on, tied up my boots, and continued with the hike. It was such a relief as I walked to have my feet slowly warm up and have feeling come back to my toes.

***

We finally arrived in a village called Upper Pisang before the rain hit later that afternoon. It was built up on a mountainside and looked over a huge valley covered in pink barley fields and horses grazing in the meadows.

Snowcapped mountains surrounded us. We could touch the clouds.

I felt tiny.

And weightless.

3300 meters above sea level.

Early the next day, Rikki and I headed out for our long and difficult, yet gorgeous, hike to Manang. Jay stayed behind and would meet us there, as he was feeling tired and wanted to take the shorter route by the road.

So, it was a girls only hike that day.

We walked along the mountain ridges almost the whole trek, up and over slopes, across dry, rocky earth.

It was tough. We trekked up quite a steep incline.

My breathing was shorter, my lungs worked harder.

We were high up, and my body was feeling it.

But did those views ever take my breath away. I felt on top of the world. We were surrounded by pine covered mountain peaks, snowy summits, and rolling valleys far below.

We were literally walking through the clouds.

The world felt so big. I felt so small.

None of my problems mattered out there.

Nothing mattered out there.

I could hear nothing but the sounds of distant rivers, the wind whistling past me, and my own heavy breathing.

Away from everything.

We kept walking up.

Up.

Up some more.

My legs felt like jelly, and my heavy bag pulled me down. My shoulders were angry at me. I had to focus on my breathing; I had to work harder and harder to fill my lungs.

Take one step at a time.

I was exhausted. And sore. I had to push myself to keep going. I could think of nothing else but each step and breath I was taking.

The cool air pinched my face.

We just kept on climbing higher. And higher. And higher. Above the clouds.

On top of the world.

Finally, that blissful moment came where we reached the top of one mountain, and came to a small village called Dgawal. Small stone houses were built high up, way in the clouds, looking down at the world.

It was silent up there.

"Oh, my god! We did it!" I cheered to Rikki as I blissfully stepped onto flatter land. I caught my breath.

She smiled as she stepped up behind me. "That means it's finally time for food!"

A break felt surely needed.

Some houses had smoke blowing out of the chimneys. A handful of local people roamed about, carrying baskets of apples and thick logs for firewood.

Prayer flags blew in the wind.

"Okay, let's see if any of these little teahouses are serving food right now."

At that moment, a frail, old lady walked out of her house carrying a large bowl. She had a long, gray braid falling down her back, and a plaid scarf wrapped around her head.

"Fresh apple pie! Do you want some fresh apple pie? I make this morning."

She opened the lid, and the smell hit us like a ton of bricks.

Fresh apple pie.

Before I knew it, Rikki and I were sitting at a picnic table outside, looking over the clouds, eating warm apple pie and sipping on hot masala tea.

We didn't speak.

We just smiled and ate.

It is definitely the little things in life.

Afterward, we continued our trek for another five hours, and a few hundred more meters up, to Manang; commonly known as the acclimatization day rest stop.

Hiking brought us up and over more and more mountain tops, and in the distance, all I could see were pink and green meadows, and mountains all the way back to the horizon. All along the trails were stacked stones and prayer flags.

It was as beautiful as it was exhausting.

"How's it going, Veronica?" Rikki joked from behind me.

Breathe in.

Breathe out.

"It's going!" I joked back. "How's your breathing going?"

"Tough," she replied. "But I'm okay. Slow and steady!"

Hours later, and what felt like a million more miles, we finally made it to Manang.

We crept into the village feeling ready to collapse at any moment.

Even though it was low season, I did expect to see more people. There were a few hikers walking around here and there, but it was quiet. Manang is one road of old log teahouses and shops. Some had smoke from fireplaces. But most seemed uninhabited.

We walked down the road, looking for any decent teahouse that was open. It all felt so still and quiet, like walking through a sleeping town. I hoped for a gas-heated shower, maybe a sink to wash my filthy clothes in. But our choices were slim.

Just give me a hot shower, and a warm bed!

"Veronica! Rikki!"

We spun around and saw Jay. He was standing there with four other hikers.

"Hey, Jay! Glad to see you made it!"

"This is Marco, Freddy, and Tony. I met them a while back. They're hiking Annapurna too!"

We all shook hands and introduced ourselves. Not only were these guys Italian, they were from Calabria; the same city my dad is from. Such a small world. Especially since they were the first Calabrians I'd ever met outside of Calabria.

Or my Nonna's house, of course.

We bonded right away.

They also had one more trekker with them, Claire, a young French woman they met along their trek.

"Okay, guys, let's seriously find a teahouse now please!" Rikki said.

So, we did. There were a few teahouses open towards the end of the road; some desperate locals thankful for a bit of business.

Hot water? Check. Warm beds? Somewhat check. Delicious food? Definitely check.

We all spent the rest of the night sitting in the empty dining hall, warming up our feet by the fireplace, playing cards, eating *chapati* and Nepalese garlic soup, and getting to know each other. We all became friends right away, bonding over the funny stories of our treks, so we decided to stick together until the pass.

In low season, seeing almost no other trekkers, I managed to find that amazing hiking group.

Sometimes travel connects you with other like-minded people; people also on an adventure. People with views and goals like yours. People who make you feel like you belong.

I felt so fortunate.

***

Day seven: Rest day!

I spent the whole day sleeping, eating tons of *chapati* and porridge, reading my book, and never once having to put on my hiking boots. I hung out with the group in the evening; we ate together and shared stories. We prepared for the next few days; buying supplies and drying our clothes. We planned for a sleep-early, wake-early routine.

I mostly spent time with Rikki though, since that was going to be our last day together.

She had a lot longer than me to do the trek, so she was planning on doing some side treks from Manang, before heading to the pass.

The rest of us were on a bit of a tighter schedule.

After dinner, Rikki and I hugged goodbye.

Only one week with this girl, but I was sad. It was difficult to imagine doing the rest of the hike without her. She had literally been at my side every day and night.

"Good luck with your journey, Veronica." She whispered in my ear as we hugged. I don't know if she meant my trekking journey, or just in life itself.

"You too, Rikki. Take care of yourself." I smiled and whipped away a tear.

That was that.

Life can be truly amazing.

Out of nowhere, people sometimes just come into your life in these utterly fateful ways, like the universe has given you a plan. You never know who might be right around the corner, who might be there to join you on your path, to teach you a lesson, or help you in some way.

And then in a blink of an eye, they will be gone again.

Isn't that what life is? Full of hello's and goodbye's? I believe it's important to trust that it's all for a reason.

**

Early the next morning, the crew and I began our trek.

It felt so cold without the warm sun out yet.

We hiked up through the clouds, over more and more rolling mountains. The valleys were wider and rockier.

There were a few bushes and pine trees, but no more colorful flowers or apple orchards.

We were definitely higher. And colder.

A few mules passed us along the trail; After Manang, there were no more roads for jeeps, so the locals had to bring supplies up the mountain by mules. It became commonplace for us to squish over to the side of a path to let a herd pass us by. As we trekked further away from Manang, there were less villages, far fewer facilities and farms, and life felt much slower.

The only problem with that is we couldn't seem to find any teahouses for breakfast.

Everything was closed or left abandoned for the slow months.

"Guys, if I don't eat soon, I'm going to faint," shouted Freddy.

"Same here!" I said.

Everyone huffed in agreement.

It was early. We were tired. We needed fuel.

We finally entered a small village; there were only three wooden houses.

One was a teahouse. Closed.

The other looked like a restaurant and farm. Closed.

"Who has extra nuts or chocolate bars in their bag?" Tony asked.

I had a stash in my side pocket for emergencies. It was becoming one.

I knew I desperately needed energy if I was to keep going. While travelling in low season can be wonderful for peace and quiet and a lack of crowds, there are also dangers to it. What if we couldn't find a place to eat? What if someone got hurt? What if someone needed to go to a hospital and there was no one around to help us?

It was a risk I knew I was getting myself into when I started, but now the reality was slapping me in the face.

My stomach rumbled.

More time passed. We trekked a few more meters up. My feet moved so slowly.

"Hello! Breakfast here! I have breakfast!"

A man shouted from up the hill. We all turned our heads and saw a young man waving at us, standing in his old, wooden barn.

"Yes, breakfast please!" I yelled up.

My stomach was growling angrily. We all sighed in relief.

We followed him around the hill. Thinking we were being led to a teahouse, he instead brought us to a small, wooden shack. There was one picnic table outside, right next to the edge of the mountain top, and inside his shack was a tiny kitchen. Fire burning oven. Tiny chimney. A wooden table covered in freshly collected eggs.

It was the coziest kitchen I had ever seen.

"What can I make for you?"

We ordered a mix of fried eggs, porridge, and *chapati* with honey.

At that altitude, fruit was a rare sight.

"So, what are your plans after the pass?" I asked.

"I think I want to explore that area for a few days," answered Claire. "I think the Upper Mustang mountains must be stunning."

"Wow, that would be so nice to see! But I think I want to hike all the way down to Pokhara. I want to see all around the Annapurna."

"I think I will take the jeep down some of it."

"I hope I will have time to do the Annapurna base camp."

"Oh, I would love to do that too!"

Everyone was on different paths and different journeys.

We all would have to part ways soon enough.

I would miss my crew, but I was also looking forward to doing some of that trek alone. Me verses the mountains. It sounded exhilarating.

A little while later, we were all scarfing down our hot breakfasts. He had cooked all of it alone. By himself, in his cute, tiny kitchen. One of the few locals sticking out low season.

We paid and said a huge thank you, and then headed up along the trail again.

We climbed up to 4250 meters high and stopped for the day in a small village called Ledar. There only seemed to be one teahouse open. Everything else was either a barn or an uninhabited wooden house. Our teahouse seemed to be a farm as well; there was a huge field of yaks right outside!

There were no shops, just our farmhouse, a few distant barns, and cloud covered mountain tops surrounding us.

It was very cold outside. Mist lightly covered all the fields, and I could see my breath.

We took turns taking a hot, gas-powered shower. I put on as many layers as I could, as we all met in the dining area. The only room with a fireplace.

"Dinner?" Marco asked.

"No, first this…" Freddy whipped out a bag of hash he got from a farmer a few days prior. Obviously, weed is not difficult to find in a country where marijuana grows like dandelions.

We all smoked together, ordered a ton of food, and spent the rest of the evening there laying on the benches, just chatting and joking around.

It was such a nice night. We had no worries, no stresses, it was like life didn't exist outside those mountains for us. We had no contact. No news updates or work emails. I wasn't even thinking about China or going back to Canada.

It was just us. Talking about our lives, our goals, our childhoods. We played games. We told funny stories.

We ordered more food.

Nothing else mattered. The only thing that mattered was hiking to the next stop tomorrow, how dry our boots were, and if we all had enough warm clothes.

There were no back-of-my-mind thoughts. No worries. No due dates or chores. No phone messages or social media notifications.

Just today.

It was like I escaped from reality.

It was an amazing feeling. A truly free feeling. It was also dangerous, because once you experience it, it's hard to go back.

***

We all woke up at sunrise and began our ninth day of hiking to High Camp. The last stop before the pass.

This day was the riskiest one.

147

After leaving Ledar, we were trekking through a mountain-side field of bushes, when we came across a herd of yak! They were standing in a field grazing and began to look right at us as we approached.

There must have been well over twenty of them.

We all stopped right in our tracks.

"Um…what do we do?" asked Claire.

"I think walk around."

"No, I think we walk through."

"Are you crazy! They're massive! We walk around."

"Walk around way up the mountain? No way it's too far!"

I was staring right at one as they argued. "Hello, Yak," I soothingly said, "can we please walk by?" I put my hand out and slowly approached it.

It stood up straighter and let out a puff of air. *Nope, never mind.*

"Veronica, are you crazy?"

Marco, Claire, and Jay began to walk up and around the herd of yaks.

Tony, Freddy, and I just stood there.

I really didn't want to walk another hundred meters up just to pass them, but I also didn't want to become a victim of a stampede.

Suddenly, Freddy lifted his poles in the air and began yelling, "Move yaks!"

And they did. They scampered away like cattle.

The other three looked down at us, astonished at Freddy.

"See? Now we walk."

We walked through the parted yaks, as they then continued grazing.

They weren't so scary after all.

After another hour of walking, we came across a river.

It was wide, and flowed quite fast. And the fallen river bed looked fresh; there seemed to be newly eroded ground next to it. And there was no bridge.

We just stood there looking confused.

"Does anyone see an area thin enough to cross?"

We all split up a bit, walking up and down the river, looking for somewhere to cross.

Up a few yards, I found a spot that looked a tad thinner than the rest of it.

"Guys! Over here!"

They walked closer.

"Is that the best we have?"

No one answered. We looked up and down again.

There was no other way across.

"I'll go first," I said, as I took off my back-pack and tossed it over.

The river was about six feet wide. Doable.

Although, I was in thick clothes. And heavy boots. And it was slippery. Morning dew still covered the grass.

I breathed in, and leaped.

My feet hit the ground, but as I fell forward, I started to slip. I grabbed some tall, piney bushes just in time. The spiky pine needles pierced into my skin, but I wouldn't let go in fear of falling into the rapid moving river.

"Careful!" yelled Claire.

I caught my breath and pulled myself up and away from the river. *Thank goodness*!

"Okay! Who's next?!"

It got easier for everyone to jump across, because there were more of us to catch them. We walked away from that river lucky; no one got soaked that day.

That's another negative aspect to low season trekking; no one around to fix the trails.

***

As we climbed further and further up, the land got much more barren, and the air got much thinner. I was lucky I didn't get a bad headache, or nausea, but it was definitely tough to breathe. I had to focus on taking slow, deep breathes, and I tried opening up my chest to let in as much air as I could.

It was difficult.

We were all trying to take it slow.

But we were also exhausted. And sore.

My back was killing me. My shoulders felt raw from the weight of carrying my back-pack for so many days strait. My leg muscles were working overtime.

It was strenuous.

I thought about Rikki a few times, hoping that she was doing well and she would be okay alone and hiking that terrain a few days later. I wished I could have contacted her somehow, just to check in.

But my goodness, by that point, was I ever getting determined to cross that pass. It was getting so close!

The terrain was rocky, and dirty, and almost lifeless. No green trees anymore. No cute farms anymore. Just distant snowy summits and ranges of barren mountains.

And it was getting colder.

The trail eventually led to a thin, mountain-side path. The mountain was covered in huge boulders and gravel. It looked completely unstable.

There was even a sign: *Danger. Keep watch for landslides.*

Oh great.

I walked two steps watching my feet, two steps looking up for dust or falling rocks. One step too far to my right and I would tumble all the way down the rocky mountain. And at any point could something fall on my head. There was nowhere else to run in case a landslide did occur.

It was the first time on the Annapurna Trek that I was truly quite scared. We all walked down that path slowly, and constantly looking up to try and spot any falling rocks or rolling boulders. Thankfully, we all made it to High Camp. No injuries. No crushed heads.

I collapsed when I got to the top.

My body was done.

My lungs were feeling weak and my body was at its limit.

My whole body was freezing cold and I couldn't feel my fingers. I was body and mind exhausted.

I was worried the altitude would make me sick overnight; I was apprehensive that I wouldn't be able to climb all the way to the pass. My breathing felt staggered and heavy just sitting there.

I just hoped I would find the energy to keep myself going.

Chapter 12

Nepal

When we wandered into High Camp, it looked almost eerie; it was quiet, seemed empty, and we could barely see the teahouse through the misty clouds engulfing us.

The rain was starting to soak my clothes.

There was one large building, surrounded by small wooden shacks. The main restaurant and the dorms I figured. We all headed straight for the restaurant. Food and a fireplace.

"How is everyone feeling?" Tony asked.

We all got comfortable on some benches circling the fireplace.

Shoes were coming off; fingers were warming themselves up. Food was getting ordered.

"I'm okay. It was hard to breathe the last little bit."

"I've got a headache."

"Drink lots of water, everyone!"

Climate sickness is unpredictable. It can hit anyone, big or small, fit or not, and can be minor with just headaches and overworked lungs, or severe with vomiting, dizziness, or migraines. We had a few headaches in the group, we all struggled to breathe deeply, but we couldn't really complain.

I felt surprised with how good I was feeling. I had a minor headache, and my lungs definitely felt the altitude, but I was prepared for worst case scenario.

I expected to get sick.

I was feeling pretty great, considering. I felt confident. I felt proud of myself.

We pigged out on whatever we thought healthiest and most filling, and spent the rest of the evening chatting by the fire.

Our rooms were freezing cold. There were no hot showers.

Just this one toasty room with a fireplace.

So of course, as more and more hikers began to arrive, they all seemed to flock toward the heat source. There were two lovely young ladies from Holland. A nice man from Korea. Two funny young guys from France. And us.

There were a couple of hikers there too, who were suffering from bad altitude sickness. One man was throwing up constantly and was curled in a ball on his bed. The other had a bad migraine and could barely keep his eyes open. We kept bringing them water, tried to get them to eat. The staff at the restaurant said they would probably have to stay an extra day and night, to acclimatize.

In that environment, so high in the mountains with no internet or roads or hospitals nearby, you just have to hope nothing serious happens.

We all ate together, talked together, warmed up together. We all got to know each other. The spicy smell of *chai* and garlic soup filled the small wooden room. Logs cracked in the fireplace.

All different people. From different countries, families, backgrounds, and ethnicities. We were all from different parts of the world.

And we were all on this hike, this adventure, with the same goal.

Instant friendships were formed.

I sat next to the fireplace under all the layers I had with me, my hands clutching a hot cup of tea, and I chatted with those fellow hikers. As good of a time as I was having, the back of my mind was worried for the hike the next day. I didn't want to get sick like the other hikers did. I didn't want to get hurt.

I just hoped I would make it safely.

***

That night, I had the worst night's sleep of my life. I kept waking up gasping for air. My lower back was killing me, I could not get comfortable and fall asleep. I think it was from my kidneys not getting enough oxygen. My lungs were burning, and my muscles were still aching.

Talking to the others about it later, it turned out everyone had a similar night.

I woke up unrested, sore, and grouchy. Even just walking a few feet felt strenuous.

How am I going to make the pass like this?!

Everyone got up with the sun, and we all drearily got ready for the hike; packing our bags and brushing our teeth outside with our water bottles.

I was one of the first gone. I was so determined to get to that pass; it was almost all I could think about. I wanted to get there before the altitude hit me even worse. The Italians were shortly behind me. Jay and Claire just after them.

It was cold. My fingers were freezing up.

I felt the struggle with breathing hit me right away. I could barely inhale. My lungs were on fire.

I took it a little bit at a time. Small, steady steps.

Up higher and higher.

Across barren ground, over frozen trails, through hazy clouds.

Breathe in. Breathe out.

It burned.

My headache was getting stronger; at times it felt like it was going to explode. I had to stop a few times to catch my breath. When Tony, Freddy, and Marco caught up, they felt the same.

But I was trying to run on my adrenaline. I knew I had to go on.

We were so close.

After a couple of hours, I crossed a rackety bridge, then up another mountain top. Then another. The sun started to come out, and it warmed up a bit.

There was not one tree. No bushes. No wildlife. Absolute empty land. Dry land. There was no sense of life up there.

The wind was cold. It stung my face like sharp prickles.

I just kept focused on my breathing. Inhaling slowly, exhaling slowly. Little steps.

Don't get dizzy.

We were well past five thousand meters high at that point.

It just never seemed to end. Every time I would get to the top of one ridge, there would be another one behind it. It went on and on and on.

How much longer can I keep hiking?

I was starting to lose all my energy.

I felt like I was just going to collapse.

Around another corner; I saw it.

Colors.

Prayer flags. Tons of them. A massive pile.

I'm here.

I saw the prayer flags, hundreds of them, wrapped and hung around the huge sign that read: *Congratulations for the Summit! Throng La Pass, 5416m.*

The biggest smile crept up on my face.

It was instant adrenaline. A rush of joy overtook me.

"Woohoo!" I stood there cheering!

There is no better feeling in the world than achieving something you worked incredibly hard for.

I had never felt more powerful.

Tony, Marco, and Freddy got closer, and they began to yell and cheer. We all hugged each other, and shouted, and laughed. We took tons of pictures.

I felt energized. No more headache or feeling cold or tired lungs.

Just pure joy.

***

Jay and Claire got there shortly after us. Then the young French guys. We all slowly made it to the pass. We all cheered each other on.

It was an accomplishment we were all proud of.

But then the adrenaline wore off, and reality hit; *we have to hike down the mountains now.*

Eleven kilometers of hiking downward. I was dreading that part.

I just wanted to get it over with. I trekked down the mountain as fast as I could. The ground was all dirt, and gravel, and rocks. It was dry and dusty. I was getting covered in dirt and dust as I hiked further and further down. I used my poles to keep myself from slipping and falling forward into a ravine.

It was tedious.

Eventually, I started to notice a pine tree here or there. A touch of green in the barren landscape. Then a few more trees. Some bushes. A patch or two of grass.

I was finally approaching livable territory again.

My lungs could breathe!

The views began to go from dull and brown, to colorful and alive. I got to the edge of one mountain and saw Mukinath way below; the town I was planning on stopping at for the night.

It was so close, yet so far.

But it was beautiful. The small town was surrounded by bright green valleys, curvy blue rivers, and surrounding snow-capped mountains. The misty clouds swirled in the blue sky.

It looked like something out of a Disney movie.

It took a few hours, but I made it to Mukinath in one piece.

I was so close to a shower, a bed, and a hot cup of tea!

It was where we all said goodbye though. Eventually everyone passed through that town. Some were continuing on to the next village, some went off to look for a jeep to take them to Jomsom, the airport town. Some stayed back to relax for a few days or even do some day treks.

I knew we would catch up again down the road, probably in the city, Pokhara.

But at that point, I was excited to be on my own for a little while.

How I like it best.

I walked into Mukinath; it was quite big compared to the villages I stayed in along the hike. Mukinath had bigger hotels, little shops and restaurants, and it was surrounded by beautiful monasteries. It was just one road like the others, but it seemed a bit livelier, and more inhabited.

I found a cool, reggae-themed guesthouse, got a private room, took a hot shower, and lay in my bed just embracing the feeling of accomplishment I had.

Those past few days were difficult. They tested and pushed me. But they were amazing. I felt so free. In my own world.

And I was already missing it.

***

Early the next day, I hit the trails again. But this time I was on my own. Both nervousness and excitement flowed through my body.

Along the trails for the whole Annapurna trek, there were these occasional little painted red signs. Whether it was on a boulder, or the trunk of a tree, they told you that you were on the right track.

I was relying on those.

I kept my eyes peeled for little red painted signs. When I would see one, I'd exhale, *Phewf! I'm not lost yet!*

The villages and main road continued down the valley, but the trails took me up and over a few mountains. It was tough, but the scenery was gorgeous.

At least I could breathe better down there.

No more empty landscape; this one was full of life. The mountains were green again. There were trees. I passed a few shepherds herding their flocks of sheep.

There was barely anyone around.

Utter peace.

A few hours into my hike, I came across very muddy land. The trail was hard to see. I looked around and saw a flat field to my right and guessed the trail must be that direction. I walked for a while, hoping to see a red sign, but never did. I walked through a forest clearing, across the muddy ground, looking desperately for some kind of sign. Any kind of hint of a path.

There was nothing.

Another ten minutes passed. Then twenty. My map didn't have very much detail. I decided to turn around and head back to the field. I retraced my steps, easy in the mud thank goodness, and found my way back to my original crossroad. I stood there staring at my map, but the trail didn't make any big turns, it just seemed to go through the mountains, to the next town. I stared straight ahead at the grassy mountains in front of me. I didn't see anything that looked like a trail, just thick grass and scattered trees.

The map indicates to head over the mountains, so I guess I should just head over the mountains.

I walked onward, just hoping I was headed in the right direction. I trekked up slowly, and over the fields at the top; sheep were grazing in the pastures, and the views of the forests down below were incredible. I kept my eyes focused up on the ridge, so I wouldn't lose my way.

When I finally got to the highest point, I looked for any sign of life on the other side.

Is that…yes…it's a road!

I saw a small road way at the bottom of the next valley, and knew I must have been on the road to Jomsom. And just when I started to doubt myself again, that's when I saw it; a small boulder with a red painted sign on it. A huge smile crept up on my face. I suddenly felt much more as ease, and enjoyed my walk down.

I listened to my music, stopped every once in a while for a water break, and just enjoyed the views.

I hiked down one mountain, crossed the valley, and hiked up the next one, where I got to small town. It was such a traditional farming village; little wooden houses, colorful vegetable gardens, barns built out of wooden logs.

It felt very little-house-on-a-prairie to me.

I spotted one woman working in her garden.

"Hello?" I said to her.

"Hello! Hungry?"

I smiled. "Yes, actually!"

"Come to my teahouse," she said as she stood up, "I make you good meal!"

She wore a soil-covered dress and her hair was loosely wrapped in a plaid scarf.

I followed her to her little stone cottage; it had a cute garden outside, and an amazing view of the mountains.

She showed me to a little table under a tree.

"This is very nice, thank you!"

She handed me a menu. I didn't even have to look at it.

"Can I please have some warm garlic soup, *chapati*, and a cup of masala tea?" I'd been eating that almost every day for lunch, but it was so tasty!

"Very good. I go make for you." And she headed off into her kitchen.

I was liking those unplanned stops; just coming across a little village in the mountains. I enjoyed the spontaneity. I was exploring the Himalayas on my own terms.

I continued to follow the trail, alongside a sandy mountain, with the wind gusting toward me. I dug my poles deep into the sand with every step, to keep myself from slipping.

It was steep.

But I saw so many red painted signs.

As long as I'm going the right way, I kept thinking.

Well those signs must have been old, because they clearly hadn't been updated in a long time. I was walking along the trail, when it just ended.

Bam. Gone.

There was nowhere else to walk. It was like the mountain I was on had been dug away or suffered a landslide. The trail went straight down a cliff.

No way to walk down; a completely vertical drop.

Just steep sand and gravel.

I looked all around me. *Am I on the right path?*

But there was no other way to go. I hadn't missed any turns or misread any signs. There used to be a path there. Now it was completely gone.

Shit.

I did not want to turn around and go back. That would have taken hours.

I walked along the cliff, looking for a way down. But there wasn't one. I kept walking and walking, getting more and more frustrated. I saw nothing but abrupt cliff ledges, and a very long way down. I hoped for any other solution but turning around and going back.

Screw that.

My back was sore and tired from carrying my bag all day, my feet were aching, the sun was beginning to sunburn my shoulders.

I finally came to a part of the cliff that didn't look as steep as the other parts. I was about twenty-five feet high, but the terrain going down looked perhaps slidable.

I stepped down, and my feet sunk into the gravel. I began to slowly slide down the hill, bit by bit, until I finally got to the main road.

I was filthy. I was sweaty. I was disgusting. My shoes were full of sand.

But I was finally there!

Jomsom was a big town made up of old, stone buildings and dusty roads, all built around a big, bright monastery. It felt quiet. The little streets were almost completely empty.

There weren't many other people there, just a few local kids riding bicycles up and down the dusty streets. There were a few little shops, but most of them were closed or even boarded up.

I walked through the empty streets, desperate to find shelter, as I felt my sweaty skin getting more and more sunburned. I guess low season sends most village inhabitants to the bigger cities for work.

There was one teahouse open, and it was home to a young, friendly couple named Kay and Tino. It was two stories high, with all the rooms opening onto the little dining area. As soon as I checked in, Kay scurried off to make me an early dinner, and Tino began to discuss with me what my plans were.

"You want to go to Pokhara?"

We were sitting at a table in the dining area.

"Yes," I answered, "that's the plan. I have to get to Kathmandu for my flight home in six days from now. And I can bus from Pokhara. So as long as I get there in the next few days."

"How will you go?"

"Well, I was thinking about taking a jeep halfway tomorrow, then taking a couple of days to walk the rest."

"But road closed for four days."

I stopped drinking my tea. "What?"

"Big landslide. No road. People can only hike it."

"Only hike? Ok…well, how long does it take to hike to Pokhara from here?"

"Hmm, maybe seven days?"

"Seven days?" I shouted. "I don't have seven days!"

"You can wait until road clears."

They said four days; but it was Nepal. It was unpredictable. It could take five, or six, or ten. Not worth the risk.

"I can't Tino, I don't have enough time. Is there another way? Another trail perhaps?"

"No. But you can take plane."

"Plane?"

"Yes, plane! Leave from Jomsom airport. Planes go to Pokhara many times a day."

An airport. In the mountains. In Nepal.

That had a *Hell No* written all over it.

"Is it safe, Tino?"

"Oh yes, very safe."

I was doubtful. "Are you sure?"

I'm not scared of flying or anything, but a small airport in the middle of a Nepalese village? Taking off from a runway surrounded by mountains? Aren't airports like those the ones you always read about on the news? *Airplane crashed into mountain while taking off.*

But he just smiled at me, "Of course, miss. Very safe. I take many times! Not many crashes at all. Very very few. Okay, I go and book for you right now!" And he got on his phone and called the airport.

It cost fifty bucks.

Sometimes it's difficult to find the line between adrenaline rushes and just plain stupidity.

***

I woke up at five the next morning, ready for my six thirty flight. I had another horrible nights' sleep; My bed felt like a slab of rock, and I was up most of the night with my mind racing. I was feeling apprehensive about the flight.

Even a little bit frightened.

I walked down the dark, empty roads, looking for that tiny airport. The whole town was still asleep.

I had no expectations for what the airport would be like. I was just hoping for some sense of security and organization.

I was not that surprised.

The airport was just one big room, full of plastic seats and a couple of desks. The check-in counters didn't even have computers, just a list of names and times. There were no metal detectors or x-ray scanners, just tables where the staff would open the customers' bags and look inside.

Both tourists and locals were crowding the desks, trying to get on the next flight to Pokhara. There were no queues, no sense of order or direction.

Just pure chaos.

I felt a mixture of amusement, and panic.

I got my ticket for a flight at six thirty, but by seven thirty I figured planes must have followed their own schedule.

There were no airplanes on the runway.

"Excuse me, do you happen to know when my flight is going to arrive?"

The man sitting at the desk looked up at me. He had disheveled dark hair and was wearing jeans and sneakers. "No, ma'am, flight leaves when plane arrives."

It was just a long waiting game.

Nothing to do but sit in uncomfortable chairs and listen to Bollywood game shows on the one TV in the airport.

Finally, two hours later, a plane landed on the runway.

Well, there we go! I thought to myself.

The airport was getting more and more packed as the morning rolled on. I was one of the very first people to arrive though, so I figured that had to be my plane.

The airplane was called.

Not mine.

Another plane landed shortly after. It was also called.

Not mine.

Feeling frustrated, I walked over to the same man sitting behind the desk.

"Excuse me, my plane was supposed to leave almost three hours ago. Why have I not been put on any of those planes?"

"You are one person. We will fill with families and tour groups first. We can put you in empty seat." He made himself look busy and walked away through the crowds.

So that was it? I was to be shoved on the plane of extras? A plane of elderly and sad, single women? Twosomes got priority over singles? That totally didn't seem fair!

I was growing irritated. I had nothing to do but walk back and forth, trying to keep myself calm. I wanted to take a good plane. Not some back up end-of-the-day plane for single people.

My nerves were getting to me.

A bit of anxiety.

Are these planes safe?

They were much smaller than airplanes I was used to. The seemed to fit only twenty people on them.

Another plane came and went.

Without me.

I was getting quite annoyed.

"Excuse me! I already paid for this plane! I was supposed to arrive in Pokhara hours ago! You keep putting families and couples on before me, it's not fair. Put me on the next plane please!"

He looked around, looking nervous and unsure of what to say.

"Um, I don't know when next plane will come."

Are you serious?

He looked down at his clipboard. "Uh, well, how about helicopter?"

I just stared at him and what he said.

Did he say helicopter?

"Oh, well, okay. That's fine I guess," I tried not to smile.

So much better than an airplane!

"Good. Helicopter leaves in ten minutes. Please go wait outside."

At that, I picked up my backpack, and rushed out onto the tarmac. There were four other tourists standing there as well. We all looked at each other and gave a mutual 'Woohoo, we are the lucky bastards that get to take the helicopter!' nod.

Just then I saw a bright yellow helicopter fly out of the clouds above, and slowly make its way around a mountain and down to the runway.

The strong wind coming from the propellers blew through my hair, and calmed my previous nerves with a new sense of excitement.

Half a dozen tourists got off with exhilarated looks on their faces.

I was excited.

Scared too. But mostly excited.

"Okay! You all go on now!" Someone on the runway yelled to us.

I speedily walked toward the helicopter first. I wanted the front seat. Screw politeness and etiquette. This was the experience of a lifetime!

I wanted the front.

The doors opened, and I jumped inside next to the pilot.

It was like sitting in a glass ball; I had a view all around me. Windows enclosed the entire helicopter.

"Seatbelts on!"

The pilot closed the hatch and turned on the propellers.

It was louder than I expected. Although I could still hear my heart pounding through my chest.

We took off.

For the next forty minutes, I flew over the Himalayas; looking down at the rolling mountains of greenery and waterfalls, rooftops in the villages, huge rivers in the valleys.

I felt like I was the one flying; I was above the world. It was truly amazing.

I will never forget that experience for the rest of my life.

***

After that, I spent the next five days in Pokhara.

It was much calmer than Kathmandu, and much prettier. The main road ran along a lakeside, covered in tall, blooming trees. The lake was full of colorful row boats and busy fishermen.

The town felt huge to me! There were guesthouses and restaurants everywhere. Coffee shops. Souvenir stores. Yoga retreats.

It was alive.

It was a perfect place for relaxation after such a long and difficult trek.

I spent my days soaking in as much of Nepal as I could before I had to leave.

I rested my tired body. I spent afternoons reading in cafes, I did yoga in the early mornings on my guesthouse's rooftop. I wandered around the lake.

I even met Jay, Marco, Freddy, and Tony a few days later when they finally made it. We grabbed some drinks one night and shared stories of our journeys to Pokhara; mine being the helicopter, theirs being a long jeep ride then a hike past landslide-covered roads.

Both exciting and story worthy.

The next thing I knew, I was packing up my bag and heading for the bus to take me to the airport in Kathmandu.

That was it. My adventure was over.

Time to go back to Canada.

It was surreal. Where did the time go?

Time is a crazy thing. We are so controlled by it. It dictates every moment in our lives; when to wake up, leave the house, head to the office, go to the gym, eat, sleep, cook, relax. Time consumes our every decision. Our every action.

But time is such an illusion. Sometimes in life, you might get lucky enough to escape it. You get to just live in moments. Eat when you're hungry. Rest when you're tired. Stop and enjoy the moment when you want to. Time doesn't really exist. It's something humans created to keep things running. To organize our days.

The present moment is the only thing that truly exists; We must learn to enjoy that fact. Don't stress about the future, don't live in the past; enjoy the moment you're living in right now. You'll never get it back again.

And that's the truth I hope to live the rest of my life by.

Appreciate and relish this current moment you're living in. Enjoy every aspect of it. Soak everything up. That's the only reality we actually have.

Chapter 13

Canada

Sometimes we all need to take a little break in life just to breathe.

That's what I was doing back in Canada. I needed a break from all the excitement and constant change, and just spend some time in a familiar place.

Spend time with my wonderful family who had waited so patiently for me.

When I arrived in Canada, my dad picked me up at the airport; greeting me with a huge smile and hug. The cold hit me like a truck! I forgot what Canadian autumn's felt like. I spent the next few weeks jumping between his house, my grandmother's, and my mom's; trying to spend time with everyone.

It's difficult to get used to people taking care of you again.

As happy as I was to be back in Ottawa, a place of comforts, familiarity, and unconditional love, I spent my first few days crying.

I was an emotional wreck.

Reverse culture shock. It's real.

Some people acted like I was just away traveling. I was away having fun, exploring the world, going on holidays.

"How were your travels, Veronica? Back to reality now, eh?"

It was frustrating.

I wasn't traveling. I was living.

I had a home. I had friends. I had a partner. I had a job. I had familiar routes to work, favorite restaurants to go to on weekends, supermarkets I would shop at. I had a bicycle I rode around on for years. I had awesome coworkers I worked with every day.

I had routines. Securities. I had a life.

I was used to chaotic cities, new faces, and petrifying bus rides. I was comfortable with the crowds, the wild landscapes, the exoticism.

I was used to not understanding anyone around me. I was familiar with getting lost.

I embraced new sights and sounds.

I was used to relying on myself.

That was, and still is, my reality. Not Canada.

Not anymore.

After a few weeks of staying in a city of simplicity and organization, I began to feel that I just didn't belong there anymore.

I wasn't the same person I was before I left.

"So, tell me sweetie, what are your plans now?" my mom poured both of us another glass of red wine, as we sat there at her kitchen table.

"I don't know…" I said as I took a sip.

She just smiled. "Come on, you can tell me. Where are you off to next?"

"Well, I think it would be nice to stay closer to home. I would like to visit once a year. Maybe South America? I need a change."

I knew it broke her heart to know I was always so far away. Like any mom, she wanted her children close by. But she knew me, more than I even knew myself, and she knew I never planned on staying in Canada permanently.

"Closer is good!" she laughed. "But don't feel guilty sweetie, you don't belong here anymore."

She took a sip of wine, and I just looked up at her in surprise.

"Really? You see it too?"

She laughed, "Of course I do! I see you walking around town, the way you look at things, the way you talk about life. You're not happy here. It's okay! I'm so proud of you...you're meant for something bigger."

It was amazing to talk to someone who saw what I felt.

It felt reassuring.

"Thanks, Mom, it really means a lot to me to hear you say that."

We hugged, and finished our wine.

***

It's weird coming home after being so far away for a long time. You are a different person, but everything else is the same.

I experienced adventures that changed me; that helped me grow stronger and more aware of the world around me. I spent years in awe, wonder, amazement. I felt frightened, alone, lost, and anxious. I cried. I laughed. I learned to trust myself.

My priorities transformed from materialism to minimalism.

My perception on life was completely different; that's what happens with each new experience.

However, everything else was the same. Ottawa felt the same as when I left. Same people, same landscapes, same lifestyle. Same routines. Same views and primacies.

But I was different.

And nobody could understand.

I didn't fit in with the people anymore; we had nothing in common. I didn't care about the things they cared about. I didn't want the lifestyle they lived. There was nothing wrong with it of course, but it just wasn't for me.

I missed living out of my suitcase.

I missed being on my own.

I missed my life.

I struggled to find my place in the world again.

I found some online teaching jobs. I spent lots of time with my wonderful family. I made sure to catch up with a few old friends. I kept practicing yoga.

I kept on writing.

I was so fortunate to have the ability to come home; somewhere safe. I had family around me who loved and missed me. We had stories to tell. We had so much lost time to catch up on.

I love my family so much. I was so lucky to be home, safe.

But I knew I couldn't stay forever.

Something else that I struggled with back home was the pressure.

In Asia, I felt free. Age didn't matter. Job position didn't matter. Finances didn't matter. When it came to travel and expat life, it didn't matter where you came from, what clothes you were wearing, or whether you were married or not. There was no judgment. Everyone just inspired each other. We supported each other. We simply enjoyed our days together.

In the Western world, it felt a bit different. I was almost thirty and not married. Almost all my friends had husbands. Some had babies. Most owned their own house, and car. I owned a backpack.

They had nice clothes. I didn't even know what was in style anymore.

They were slowly checking off all the boxes society bestows upon us. The only list I was checking off was my travel one.

It felt so strange, because I never cared about that stuff while I was in Asia. But back home, it filled my every thought. It fueled my insecurity.

The rat race; it's one reason I stayed away for so long.

I knew it was all in my head, but I felt like I didn't have much to show for my years. I had stories, sure, but I didn't own anything. I wasn't married. I had no kids. I barely had money saved in my bank account. My life had been devoted to travelling; to experiences and adventures. I had never even thought about buying a home or settling down.

Here, I did.

It worried me.

Back in Cambodia, or China, or even traveling in some far-away country, I felt powerfully independent. I was brave, and fierce. I felt strong. I took care of myself.

I had a purpose.

In Canada, I was taken care of. I stayed with my family, under their roofs. I ate from their kitchens. Hell, even my license had long ago expired, so they had to drive me around from place to place.

I felt like a nobody there.

I felt truly lost for the first time in a long time.

What am I doing with my life? Where is home supposed to be?

A few weeks into my time back in Canada, I decided it was time to plan my next step. My next journey.

I was still figuring out what I wanted, but I definitely knew what I didn't want.

I tackled Asia quite well. I thought it might be time for a new continent. A new adventure.

Home is not just a roof and four walls. Home is where you feel safe. Where you feel comfortable. Where you feel the most you.

Maybe that isn't a single place for some people; maybe it's the road.

I'm going to enjoy this time with my family; some time to breathe. Time to rest my mind.

But I can't wait to go home again.

CPSIA information can be obtained
at www.ICGtesting.com
Printed in the USA
LVHW011040100721
692363LV00024B/902

9 781947 353329